# *Who They Really Were*

## Preaching On Biblical Personalities

## John R. Bodo

CSS Publishing Company, Inc., Lima, Ohio

Scripture quotations are from the *New Revised Standard Version of the Bible*, copyright 1989 by the Division of Christian Education of the National Council of the Churches of Christ in the USA. Used by permission.

Scripture quotations are from the Revised Standard Version of the Bible, copyrighted 1946, 1952 ©, 1971, 1973, by the Division of Christian Education of the National Council of the Churches of Christ in the USA. Used by permission.

**Library of Congress Cataloging-in-Publication Data**

Bodo, John R.
    Who they really were : preaching on biblical personalities / John R. Bodo.
       p.    cm.
    ISBN 0-7880-1540-0 (pbk. : alk. paper)
    1. Biographical preaching. 2. Bible—Biography—Sermons. 3. Sermons, American.
I. Title.
BV4235.B56 B63 2000
251—dc21                                         99-053305

This book is available in the following formats, listed by ISBN:
    0-7880-1540-0   Book
    0-7880-1541-9   Disk
    0-7880-1542-7   Sermon Prep

*To my wife, Mary Lindstrom Bodo,*
*whose encouragement of my ministry*
*both as a preacher and as a writer*
*has been unfailing*

# Table Of Contents

# Foreword

So far as I can recall, I discovered preaching on biblical personalities by myself. I do not remember having it pointed out to me as a particularly promising option in any one of my homiletics courses. I suppose I stumbled into my discovery because I found myself intrigued and moved by a number of such sermons as far back as my seminary days. Only one comes to mind, though: a profoundly stirring sermon on Joseph of Arimathea, presented as a cultured, wealthy Princeton resident who meant well but played it safe. To this day I am grateful to the late Elmer G. Homrighausen, Dean of Princeton Theological Seminary, for his provocative interpretation.

I owe a special debt, however, to Dr. Faris Daniel Whitesell whose little book, *Preaching on Biblical Characters* (Grand Rapids: Baker House, 1955), while long out of print, is still the handiest introduction to the subject. Nearly one half of Whitesell's book examines the pulpit ministry of a few great nineteenth and early twentieth century preachers, which dates the work. But his short chapters on the why and how of such preaching have been of real help to me.

# Introduction

There are endless, dispiriting statistics about the membership losses of America's mainline churches, but I know of no reliable statistics to account for these ongoing losses. What are the reasons?

Television is certainly one of the reasons: the spell of the tube and its destructive effect on our attention span. There is also a widespread crisis of authority in our society expressing itself in mistrust of all traditionally authoritative institutions. The family, the school, the government are prime targets — along with the church. In addition, there is a more quiet but deep-seated crisis of belief in God — in a God who does not seem even to care, let alone do anything, about genocide or the ravages of the drug plague or the suffering of millions of malnourished people, even in our superrich country.

But in the midst of this dismal scene, there are growing, flourishing congregations within our mainline denominations. What accounts for their health and strength when the majority of otherwise similar churches are barely surviving? There must be many factors, of course, but I am willing to wager, without citing or even consulting any statistics, that imaginative, biblically-grounded, relevant preaching is a major factor.

The gospel is good news, the best news by far even after twenty centuries, perhaps more so than ever at a time when we have developed the capacity for destroying, literally and with finality, the marvelous planet God has given us for our habitat. This gospel is still being proclaimed in a number of ways, in fact, in many more ways than the Apostle Paul could have foreseen. But for some reason the original broadcast medium, preaching, continues to be uniquely effective — *if done well*. Thus the major obstacle to the hearing of the gospel may be neither television, nor the crisis of authority, nor the waning of belief, nor yet our hardness of heart, though we dare not belittle the power of sin. The major obstacle may be something far more prosaic: *dullness.*

The message about God's reconciling love, enfolded in that amazing library of Hebrew and Christian writings we call the Bible and enfleshed in the unique person of Jesus of Nazareth, is breathlessly exciting, endlessly varied, uncannily contemporary. It may seem impossible to dull its lustre, its keen edge. But it can be done and it is being done, and for every layman or woman who good-naturedly puts up with boring sermons, there are many more who have given up and quit.

The purpose of this little book is to help preachers preach livelier, more arresting, more memorable sermons. During four decades as a pastor-preacher and a teacher of practical theology, it has been my experience that attention to our preaching can be greatly increased and the sermon's memorability enhanced if the subject is a person, a biblical character. Preaching on biblical personalities neither rejects nor favors any of the classic "types" of preaching: textual, topical, expository, pastoral, doctrinal. What distinguishes the type of preaching I present and advocate in this book is that it focuses on one (or more than one) of the Bible's large and colorful cast of characters.

I have found this type of sermon exhilarating to prepare as well as of far-above-average appeal to congregations; hence, I am devoting the opening chapter to the *rewards* of preaching on biblical personalities.

In the second chapter, I am examining the other side of the coin (since all well-behaved coins must have two sides) by exploring some of the *pitfalls* of such preaching.

A third chapter, on some of the methods and techniques of the *preparation* of sermons on biblical characters, completes Part One.

In Part Two, I present twelve full-length sermons on personalities from both the Old and the New Testament. I hope to illustrate and to vindicate my belief in the validity and helpfulness of the approach. Each sermon is prefaced by an Introductory Note: a few words out of my workshop addressed to colleagues laboring in their workshops. The sermons are not in any particular order, nor do they claim any thematic unity. The selection is meant only to exhibit as wide a variety of sermons of this type as I have been able to conceive over the years.

Part Three contains four "brainstorms" on as many additional biblical personalities. A brainstorm is defined, for our purposes, as a collection of "angles," approaches to the character, ways to go with him/her. The object is to stimulate the reader's imagination, to encourage him/her to develop the most appealing angle into a full-blown sermon, or to continue the brainstorm on his/her own until the optimum angle appears.

I repeat: the purpose of this book is to help my fellow ministers add spice to the pulpit fare they serve up week after week. We are called to bring the scriptures to *life* for God's people. Preaching on biblical personalities is one *lively* way to do it.

# Part One

*Preaching On Biblical Personalities*

# 1. Rewards

Let us begin by reviewing some of the rewards that await us when preaching on biblical personalities.

The first reward I have found is the abundance of *instantly identifiable* material fairly begging to be used. When you are expected to preach about 48 times a year, it seems natural that you will be at a loss sometimes as to what subject to choose for your next sermon — a predicament most likely to occur during the lengthy Trinity Season. Of course, if you follow a lectionary, you are safe, but some of us have never jumped on the bandwagon. For my part, I jumped on, but it turned out to be a brief ride. Perhaps it was my fault but I found the system too confining. For me, whenever the problem of what to preach next Sunday raised its frowning head, I could smile it away by calling on one of the many biblical characters standing in line at my study door, nearly beating it down with their clamorous "Take me! Take me!"

There are in the Bible some 250 major characters and at least as many minor ones just waiting to be discovered or recalled. The adjectives major and minor do not necessarily refer to their historic or theological significance any more than the Minor Prophets are meant to be less significant than the Major Prophets. All I am implying is that some 250 biblical personalities (e.g., Abraham, Joseph, David, Jeremiah, Simon Peter, Saul/Paul) are amply documented, while we may possess very little biographical information about the others. Nevertheless, there is first-class preaching material even in many of the Bible's one-liners.

Consider Alexander the coppersmith. Alexander is mentioned in only one place, in 2 Timothy 4:14-15. Here is all he rates: "Alexander the coppersmith did me great harm; the Lord will requite him for his deeds. Beware of him yourself, for he strongly opposed our message." Here is a man who got into the Bible just because he was mean to Saint Paul! Otherwise he is an enigma. His name is Greek, but most Jews living in the Diaspora had a

Greek name in addition to their Jewish name (e.g., Saul *aka* Paul), and Alexander was surely a Jew — and a coppersmith. That is all we are told about him. The rest is Sherlock Holmes work neatly cut out for you. You'll have to decide whether Paul wrote this letter personally or whether it was written, perhaps much later, by one of his disciples, which would make a real difference in your further investigation of Alexander. The scholars, lacking consensus, are letting you be the judge. You'll have to decide, from the context as well as by dipping into early Christian history preserved in extra-biblical sources, when and where Alexander lived and what his beliefs were which caused him to oppose the gospel, or at least Paul's version of the gospel. Above all, you'll have to decide what instruction may be hidden in the fact that Alexander has been preserved for us in the Word of God in spite of (or maybe because of) his rejection of the gospel (or the gospel according to Paul). Anyone who would be mentioned by Paul or the Pauline author as having done Paul "great harm" would at least be a force to be reckoned with, and would have enlisted followers, and so on. You take it from here!

No doubt the greatest reward in preaching on biblical personalities rests in its *irresistible appeal*, because people are more interested in *people* than in anything else in the world.

During the last half-century, slick magazines have been dying like flies during the first frost. *Time* and *Newsweek* are two shining exceptions, because they follow an unbeatable formula: they begin every story, whatever the subject — politics, business, art — with a person and wrap the story around that person. But the greatest publishing success of this half-century is the magazine with the name that makes our point: *People*. It has been suggested that the finest historian is he or she who makes history read like gossip. *People* magazine lays no claim to recording history. It presents snappily written, richly illustrated gossip. But for millions of Americans it is living American history.

So let us not be snobs about gossip. The Bible itself grew out of a large body of folk tales. The great stories of Genesis 1 through 11, followed by the epics of the Patriarchs and the story of Moses, date back to preliterate times. Before they were ever committed to writing, they were gossiped around campfires and village wells and rehearsed in the people's slowly evolving religious ceremonies. But what kept them alive, what accounted for their endless fascination, was the people — Adam, Abraham, Joseph, Moses — whose walk with God (or away from God) they were recording and passing on from generation to generation.

Jesus himself was a matchless storyteller, thoroughly imbued with the stories of his people. Jesus knew that his hearers would listen more closely and be more deeply involved if he presented his teaching in the form of a story, a story about people like themselves. His Parables are, undeniably, the greatest sermons ever preached. "The land of a rich man brought forth plentifully ..." "There was a man who had two sons ..." "Two men went up to the Temple to pray ..." In his Parables, Jesus left to us a marvelous roster of characters who are also grist for our sermon mill!

Preaching on biblical personalities need not be limited to historic personages. In many instances, scholars do not even agree as to whether a certain biblical character was an historic person or a representative of his people (Abraham? Moses?) or a mythological character (Noah?). The Word of God within God's written Word is not bound by historicity. Literary figures, like the characters in the Parables of Jesus or the personalities that emerged from early Hebrew story, are all fair game for the type of preaching we are discussing. The Parables in particular are a treasure trove for the making of sermons that seek the contours of a Christian life style for a world radically different from the one Jesus faced. Rooted in their time and place, the genius of Jesus endowed them with immortality. The Good Samaritan, the Prodigal Son, the Pharisee and the Publican shall endure for our instruction, rebuke, upbuilding, as long as humankind endures.

But Jesus validates preaching on biblical personalities in an even more profound sense. Jesus favored biographical preaching in his ministry but he also embodied, in his person, God's once-and-for-all biographical sermon addressed to us, "the Word (was) made flesh ... full of grace and truth." According to the biblical story, God tried for centuries to communicate his will and his love to his people, Israel. He sent them his Law, through Moses. He sent them messages of warning and of comfort, through the prophets. Always as one removed, through a third person. At last, God wearied of being misunderstood, or disobeyed altogether. "Perhaps they will listen," God thought, "if I go to them myself, not in a scroll or a sermon, but in the form of a man...." Thus Jesus of Nazareth, God's message of love enfleshed, preaching from the midst of life with his own life....

Preaching on biblical personalities is also rewarding because it forces both preacher and people to *deal with the Bible* at some depth. By the time you have begun really to dig into the background, the beliefs, the actions of a biblical person, you are hooked. There will be no newspaper editorial, no article admirably suited for *Parents* or *Psychology Today*, from the pulpit this week. Instead of dangling from a biblical text by the thinnest of threads, this sermon will bring at least one biblical person and story to life, in the fullness of his or her context in Scripture. The congregation will appreciate it, too. They will look more alert because they will be more involved, caught up in the world of God's Word, thanks to meeting a biblical woman or man at an adult level. Some may even go home to do some reading in the Bible on their own!

One aspect of this reward, that preaching on biblical personalities compels us to deal with the Bible as adults, is that it makes the preaching and the understanding of *doctrine easier and more attractive*. It is desperately important to be able to account for what we believe and what we do not believe. To suggest that it does not matter what we believe as long as we are sincere is absurd: Hitler was utterly sincere. To hold that it does not matter what we believe as long as we lead a good life is another bromide. Who is to define that good life? Who is to judge our performance? What will hold us to it? Cut flowers fade fast. Behavior that is not grounded in a well-thought-out body of convictions is untrustworthy, at least for the long run. That is why we are supposed to preach as well as teach the doctrine, the authoritative interpretation of Scripture, of our Church.

But doctrine makes hard reading and even harder hearing. Paul's letter to the Christians at Rome is probably the greatest theological treatise ever written, but it is rough going even with Bible and commentary in hand. Romans 5 has only 21 verses, but if we expect people to follow it with the "naked ear," we are expecting too much, even though the chapter contains one of the noblest expositions of what we believe about human sin, divine forgiveness, and the Cross at the juncture of the two. Try reading it to your congregation some Sunday, the whole chapter, but be mindful of all those glazed stares!

For contrast, recall Jesus' treatment of the same central theme in Luke 7:36-50. The teaching is introduced by a dramatic occurrence. While a guest in the house of Simon the Pharisee, "a woman who is a sinner" (Mary Magdalene?) anoints Jesus with perfume. This alone is likely to wake people up, just as it did when it happened. The good people around Simon's dinner table are shocked at the outcast intruder and ready to throw her out. Jesus, however, rises to her defense and uses the opportunity for teaching his friends a lesson — in the form of a story: "A certain creditor had two debtors...." The woman gets the message and feels like a human being, a child of God, perhaps for the first time in her adult life. Simon and his guests are brought up short. They learn more about human sin and divine grace, about their own smugness and God's infinite compassion in five minutes than we are likely to learn from a full semester's work on Romans! No, I am not arrogantly belittling Paul's genius. I am merely underscoring my conviction that preaching on biblical personalities, historic or literary, can greatly enhance our communication of Christian doctrine.

Preaching on biblical personalities is rewarding also because it *dispenses with the need for illustrations.* Having confessed that I never formed a lasting friendship with any lectionary, I might as well confess another lifelong shortcoming: I have always found it difficult to find appropriate illustrations. What I did find usually struck me as too pat or too far-fetched. More than once I would write a fresh sermon around old illustrations, because I was unable to come up with any suitable new ones. Unless your mental computer has an exceptional anecdote-storage facility, you may feel at least some sympathy for my predicament.

But when you are preparing a sermon on a biblical character, this problem is not likely even to arise, because the story will function as a life-sized illustration! Your hearers will be so caught up in the actions and changing fortunes of the hero (or anti-hero), that they will not feel the need for any other, extraneous stories. Can you imagine "illustrating" the Parable of the Prodigal Son?

Another reward of this type of preaching is that it *requires a minimum of "preaching."*

As ministers of the Word of God, we may not realize how distasteful "preaching" is to most unchurched and half-churched people or even to many faithful, perceptive, sophisticated members. Think of the word with the accent your teenager uses when cutting you off with the defiant cry, "Stop 'preaching' at me!"

Preaching can be an exercise in belaboring the obvious. Preaching can be a putdown: someone standing in the pulpit, several feet above you who are seated, acting superior and making you feel inferior. Preaching can be moralizing: all whining voices and wagging fingers have not been retired. Of course, no one *means* to belabor the obvious, or put down his or her congregation, or moralize. But the medium of preaching does carry a lot of ballast from the Victorian Era and from Frontier America. It may therefore be wise for us to make sure that no one listening to our sermons will ever be screaming at us, silently, "Stop 'preaching' at me!"

Preaching on biblical personalities, I have found, gives us the best chance to let the Word of God speak for itself, with a minimum of "preaching" in the objectionable sense of the word. This potential for laying it on thin is especially helpful when the subject matter is sticky. For example, it may be impossible to preach about sexual promiscuity without either remaining too timidly general or coming across "preachy." *Looking for Mr. Goodbar* was a powerful "sermon" on the subject, in its own way, but like all sermons without the gospel, it offered no hope.

But sexual promiscuity can be dealt with from the pulpit without either self-consciousness or holier-than-thou sermonizing. Consider the story of the Samaritan woman (John 4:7-42). The woman feels soiled and worthless, like a cheap cut of meat, but she cannot talk about it. Even when Jesus baldly identifies her condition, "... you have had five husbands, and he whom you now have is not your husband ..." she tries to change the subject. But when Jesus

20

reveals himself to her, she realizes that she is lost — and saved. Accepted by Jesus, she is ready to accept herself and to begin a new life as a witness to his grace and power.

The story makes its point by telling us about a person who was sexually promiscuous and hated herself for it, but who found in Jesus the strength to change. No need to belabor the obvious, to torment any hearers whom the shoe may fit, to expound upon the perils of "riotous living." In this age of AIDS, more than ever, telling the story of this woman and letting the story speak for itself seems best.

As a matter of fact, we have in the Bible a wonderful illustration of how a story which makes its point clearly and memorably can be devalued by "sermonizing." Jesus' Parable of the Sower (or, rather, of the Seeds) is on record, with typical brevity and pungency, in Matthew 13:1-9. But the labored explanation of the story (Matthew 13:18-23) seems as unfortunate as it is unnecessary!

Finally, preaching on biblical personalities is rewarding because, having done your research well and kept abundant notes, you have probably garnered *materials for up to half a dozen more sermons*. For major, that is, well-documented characters this is obvious: if you do a thorough study of the life of David or of Simon Peter, you will have sermons to spare. But there is likely to be more than one sermon in the life story of even minor, more sketchily drawn characters, including some of those priceless one-liners — like Alexander the coppersmith.

# 2. Pitfalls

These are some of the many rich rewards of preaching on biblical personalities. But the coin does have a reverse side. This type of preaching, like every other kind, has some special pitfalls.

For one thing, it is possible to preach on biblical characters and be boring. It is not easy, because biblical people are incredibly diverse, individual, quirky. But it can be done. A sermon about a woman or man in the Bible may come off like an expanded entry from any standard dictionary of the Bible. The bones may not be fully clothed with flesh and keep rattling around. Or else, while the person is vividly recreated, he or she may remain too remote for anyone today to identify with. When that businessman in the pew should be saying to himself, "The pastor thinks that he is preaching about Zaccheus but, God help me, he is really preaching about me!" he might be thinking instead, "What a waste of time hearing about this little old man with whom I have nothing in common!" Sermons about biblical personalities require imagination. We must be able imaginatively to enter their skin, their context, their world. Likewise we must be able imaginatively to relate their experience to the experience of our hearers.

The opposite pitfall in preaching on biblical personalities is letting our imagination run riot. We are not expected to be Cecil B. DeMille or even David Lean conjuring up panoramas of the sun-scorched, hotly shimmering Near East in Technicolor and Vistavision. Creating a vivid physical setting for the story is important, but it is no more than a means to an end. Similarly, physical details about our hero or heroine, which we have to invent since usually none are given, may be carried to excess. Making biblical people too concrete in the minds of our hearers may diminish the impact of their struggle with God or witness to God, when it is that impact we are seeking to midwife and to maximize. It is one thing to get to know a biblical character in the fullness of her or his humanity. It is something else to get so artificially close to, so

23

chummy with, the character that the story might as well be another episode in a television serial.

Another pitfall in preaching on biblical personalities is really twin pitfalls. Let us call them hero worshipping and villain hissing.

The Bible is full of men and women of exceptional moral stamina and spiritual power. Just recall Hebrews 11 for an inspiring roster. Their very excellence, however, poses a problem for preaching on them. It is this: as people who lived long ago and in a world quite different from ours, they are necessarily strange to us. This is part of the challenge: to bring them closer, to make them real as flesh-and-blood, individual human beings. But if we are unduly impressed with their spiritual and moral prowess, we shall make them into saints (which some of them have come to be called, unfortunately) and thus remove them even further from our hearers.

We also need to remember that our responsibility, as ministers of the Word of God, is to exalt God: not Moses, not David, not even "Saint" Paul. There is a warning here even for our treatment of Jesus, God's own Self in human flesh. The flesh of Jesus, we need to bear in mind, was human, completely human. Therefore we serve our function of heralds of the gospel poorly, if we have Jesus walk, as the Gospel of John tends to do, several feet above the ground. Docetism was one of the earliest and most dangerous heresies in the Early Church. Docetists claimed that Jesus only seemed human (from the Greek *dokeo* — to appear, to seem). This would make him a visitor from Olympus in disguise, like Zeus in one of his many disguises. It would also make a charade of his Crucifixion and a "special effect" of his Resurrection.

In other words, we should not make a "saint" even of Jesus, let alone of any other biblical personality. We should present Jesus in the fullness of his humanity, accepting his hunger and thirst, his anger and joy, his loneliness and stubborn trust in God as evidence of the reality of the Incarnation. And if we refuse to succumb to Docetism in our treatment of Jesus, we should the more resolutely refuse to hero-worship other biblical characters for whom no claim to being superhuman has ever been entered. To be sure, Paul addresses the congregation in Corinth as "called to be saints." They were called to be saints. So are we all, once we respond to God's call through Jesus Christ. But to think of those Corinthian Christians, or of Paul himself for that matter, as saints, in the colloquially reverent sense of the word, is absurd.

Thus hero-worshiping biblical characters is a temptation to guard against. But so is treating some of them as villains beyond the ken of God's love, beyond redemption. Three men come to mind at once, all three from the Gospels. They are presented in the Gospels as people more complex, more richly human, more plausible than we have usually allowed ourselves and our congregations to perceive them.

Herod the Great (40-4 B.C.) richly deserved the epithet "great," even though most of our people know him only from the story of the Massacre of the Innocents (Matthew 2:16-17). Appointed king of the Jews after serving as governor of Galilee, Herod retained the trust and friendship of the Romans through all the convulsive power plays which marked the course of the Empire during his reign. He built magnificent cities, like Caesarea Maritima in honor of the Emperor Augustus, but he crowned his building endeavors by re-building the Temple, beginning in 20 B.C. — the Temple Jesus knew and criticized. Throughout his reign, Herod kept the Roman yoke as light as he could on his people's neck. Of course he was an oriental despot, but he was abler and apparently even kinder than most. Nor can the story of his murdering all those babies in Bethlehem be confirmed from any source outside Matthew's Gospel, even though Herod did commit atrocities against others who threatened his rule. In sum, there is a great deal more to Herod than a villain to hiss and boo. Our preaching will be enriched if we do a decent bit of Sherlock Holmes work on him and then share our findings frankly with our people.

Caiaphas also comes to mind. The son-in-law of Annas, he succeeded his father-in-law as High Priest in 18 A.D. and was thus involved in the trial and sentencing of Jesus. Not only is Caiaphas debited with speeding Jesus to his death, but the Evangelist John quotes him as saying to the Sanhedrin, "... it is expedient for you that one man should die for the people and that the whole nation should not perish" (John 11:50).

Here again we have been hissing and booing a biblical character as an unrelieved villain — without understanding him in his historic context. Caiaphas was a Sadducee, a member of the high-priestly class, pro-Roman in politics, liberal in religion, at least compared with the Pharisees. By cooperating with the Romans, the Sadducees — like Herod the Great — kept themselves safe and rich, but they also protected their people. The one thing they could not tolerate, because the Romans would not stand for it, was revolution, and there were plenty of Zealots and other would-be rebels against Rome to worry them.

Caiaphas did not know Jesus, nor what he was about. He only knew that Jesus might be one more revolutionary whom the Jews, living precariously under their Roman masters, could not afford. Perhaps Caiaphas should have investigated Jesus further. He might have become a secret sympathizer like two of his colleagues on the Sanhedrin, Nicodemus and Joseph of Arimathea. But even then Caiaphas' counsel would likely have been the same because, among the Jewish authorities, the buck stopped on his desk and because, from the standpoint of safety from Roman reprisals, it was expedient "... that one man should die for his people, and that the whole nation should not perish." Just remember what happened in 70 A.D. when, after one more Jewish revolt, the Romans said, "That is enough!" and brought destruction to the Temple and a bloody end to the Jewish state. Clearly, Caiaphas deserves a more thorough, more discerning treatment than what we usually mete out to simple villains.

The third and obvious case is Judas. I have never been able to accept the facile hypothesis that Jesus picked Judas because the plot called for a villain. The theory that Judas betrayed Jesus, because he wanted to precipitate a crisis that would force Jesus to declare himself as the Messiah and to start using his supernatural powers for the establishment of his Kingdom, is far more plausible. In addition, Judas' abysmal remorse is on record. What more could he do to show it than what he did — by committing suicide? Nevertheless, in spite of the complexity of Judas' character, motivation, action, we tend to let him remain a caricature, a cardboard villain with whom we, of course, have nothing in common. This is where the pitfall is deepest. By treating the Herods and Caiaphases and Judases of the Bible as mere villains to be hissed and booed, we neutralize their potential impact on us, since we are unable to identify with paragons: with a paragon of virtue or with a paragon of evil!

These are some of the pitfalls of preaching on biblical personalities. They are far outweighed by the rewards of such preaching. But to reap the reward and sidestep the pitfalls, it is necessary to prepare oneself thoroughly, perhaps more thoroughly than for any other type of preaching. Thus we now turn to the discipline and problems of preparation. Just one fair warning: Sherlock Holmesing biblical personalities is so much fun, it is addictive!

# 3. Preparation

## Groundwork

Preparation for preaching on biblical personalities is, in most respects, similar to preparing any other type of sermon. It is likely, however, to require both more extensive and more sharply focused research. Thus, at the risk of being obvious, I shall suggest the following stages or steps.

(1) Read the article on your character in any standard dictionary of the Bible, for example: *Harper's Bible Dictionary* (Harper and Row, 1985); *Hastings' Dictionary of the Bible*, (rev. ed., Scribner's, 1963); *The New Westminster Dictionary of the Bible*, (Westminster, 1970); or *The Interpreter's Dictionary of the Bible* (4 volumes, Abingdon, 1962). Pay attention to the character's name or names: one of them may hide an important clue. Note, for example, that my whole sermon on the Apostle Thomas hinges on his nickname, Didymus. Others undergo symbolically significant name changes, e.g., Abram to Abraham. And there is always Simon/Peter/Cephas: "Mr. Rock" (Matthew 16:18).

(2) Next, read all the biblical references to the character listed in the dictionary article. One of them may emerge as your key text. One or more of them will be your scripture lesson(s). But do not decide prematurely. Your task, at this stage, is to be a sponge, soaking up everything you can find out about your subject.

(3) Returning to the dictionary of the Bible, follow up all geographical references and all references to other persons (e.g., for Absalom, David), groups (e.g., Scribes) and social institutions (e.g., Roman Empire) which you have gleaned in the biblical readings. Place names, too, like the names of persons, often have symbolic meaning, e.g., Bethlehem means "House of Bread," the birthplace (according to Christian legend) of him who will call himself the "Bread of Life" (John 6:35). All these references can prove important for re-creating the historical and human context of the character you are seeking to bring to life.

(4) You may also find it stimulating to re-read the biblical passages from a different translation. For instance, if your initial reading was from *The Revised Standard Version*, you might benefit from turning to a less literal but equally responsible translation like the *The New Jerusalem Bible*, (Doubleday, 1985) or *The Revised English Bible*, (Oxford, 1989).

(5) Last but not least, review the biblical passage or passages you have decided to deal with in a couple of standard Bible commentaries, like *Harper's Bible Commentary*, (ed. by James L. Mays, Harper, 1988),or *The Layman's Bible Commentary*, (25 volumes, ed. by Balmer H. Kelly, John Knox, 1959-64), or *The Interpreter's One-Volume Bible Commentary*, (ed. by Charles M. Laymon, Abingdon, 1971). The only reason I hesitate to recommend the twelve-volume *New Interpreter's Bible*, (Abingdon, 1994) is that, at this stage, the excellent "Reflection" sections in the *New IB* may short-circuit your Sherlock Holmes work. Input from another preacher's mind may put out such creative sparks as may be about to issue from your mind before they have a chance to kindle a proper fire. Sampling the treatment of your biblical personality by other pulpiteers is best left to the last and may not be needed at all.

## Construction

Construction of a sermon on a biblical character is, again, not fundamentally different from constructing any other type of sermon, nor must the technique of outlining or any other technique ever become an end in itself. Nevertheless, a carefully crafted outline will go a long way toward catching and keeping the attention of the hearers.

A *straight-life outline* may seem to lack challenge, but it presents the character as completely as the available sources permit, it is easy to follow (like an old-time movie with a beginning, middle, and end), and it is gratifying because it makes people feel that they have made a new acquaintance or discovered fresh and intriguing data about an old friend. The sermon on Jonah follows a simple, chronological outline, except for tagging the three stages in the story alliteratively "disobedience," "disapproval," and "disappointment." Insofar as the Book of Jonah, the book named after its anti-hero, Jonah, *is* a story, it is appealing to retell it in story form, from "Once upon a time" to "And they lived happily ever after," even though this story has a far more subtle, ambiguous, provocative ending.

But there are any number of other ways to construct a sermon on Jonah. One way we may call *topical*. We take a topic from the life story of the character and concentrate on that topic, using the character as the major and, most likely, sole illustration. On the topic of God's freedom, we might try to point out that (a) God is free to go into action anywhere, e.g., in the Third World, among people we hardly know or can barely stand; that (b) we are not assured of God's unbroken, uncritical favor just because we are sons and daughters of Abraham or Luther or Calvin; and that (c) no people, no human being is beyond the pale of God's concern and free, redemptive love. For a title, consider "Revival in Nineveh."

Another topic from the Book of Jonah might be that colorful, unwelcome "God-Appointed Worm." The outline might be: (a) God may be testing us by gifts both welcome and understandably unappreciated like the broiling sun or the sneaky work or the "sultry east wind"; (b) we dare not pick and choose among God's commands, obeying only those that suit us; and (c) God owes us nothing, we owe God everything. Having no credit rating with God, we can at least try to be thankful debtors.

Still another topic from Jonah: "The Cost of Truthfulness." The outline might be: (a) Jonah lied to the captain about his reason for wanting to go to Tarshish, otherwise he might not have been taken on as a passenger; (b) in the storm, Jonah proved man enough to confess his guilt and to expose himself to the consequences; (c) lying is always a risky business. We may have to lie sometimes to avoid grave danger to ourselves or others. Lying to ourselves is far more dangerous, because we come to believe our own lies. Lying to God is not only dangerous: it is absurd. God knows — and lets us know he knows.

Another useful way to outline a sermon on a biblical personality may be called *propositional*. To use this method, it is necessary to be able to sum up the emerging sermon in a single sentence or proposition about the character or the chosen topic related to the character. Then we proceed to *question* the proposition with any one of the six little words of journalism: Who? What? When? Where? Why? How? The last two are likely to work best.

For example: "God loves our enemies. *Why?*" Because (a) God is also their Creator. Because (b) they may be as open to God as we claim to be. And because (c) God wants to be their Redeemer, too.

Another example: "God wants us to love our enemies. *How?*" (a) By resisting the temptation to generalize about them and, in so doing, depersonalize, dehumanize them. (b) By being open to the possibility that they can be reached, at least by God, and that they can change. (c) By welcoming and seeking contact with them even at the risk that our overtures may be misunderstood by them as well as by our friends.

### Finding An Angle

Having shown several ways to structure a sermon on a biblical character, I want to add an elusive but, in my experience, all-important ingredient: the *angle*.

What do I mean by angle? I do not mean a gimmick, though if you do not like a particular angle, you will no doubt call it a gimmick. The sermon on "Demetrius' Brother" is admittedly vulnerable to this accusation. I am prejudiced, of course. I believe that the treatment is valid, even though the angle is rather unusual. But I will have to let you be the judge.

Meanwhile I define "angle" as we use the word in the phrase, "Now let's look at this from a different angle." Recall that, in ancient Egyptian paintings and drawings, all persons appear in profile. These early artists did not know how to draw a human face *en face*. Now imagine what would happen if you could peel Pharaoh off the wall or from the side of the ornate casket and look at him frontally. You would be looking at an entirely different person, one you had never seen before! That is what I mean by an angle: revealing the biblical character from a fresh, unsuspected point of view. It cannot be done every time, but when it is done it can add a great deal of zest to the sermon.

A few examples, in the form of thumbnail sketches.

**Noah.** According to the story, humankind had so dreadfully "messed up" that, by the time Noah came on the scene, God was sorry that he had ever made Man and decided to wipe out the human race. Fortunately for us, there was Noah: one person God was not sorry to have made. Do you think God may be sorry he made you? How could you tell? Would you care? Should you?

**Zacchaeus.** Expensive and frivolous gift items are sometimes advertised as for "the man (or woman) who has everything." Zacchaeus had everything — or did he? What did he lack? How did Jesus meet his unacknowledged need?

**John Mark.** As a spoiled brat, he sorely tried the patience of his uncle, Barnabas; of Paul, who refused to take him back after he had gone AWOL; and probably of Peter, too, before Peter ever came to call him "my son, Mark" (1 Peter 5:13). If your teenager exasperates you, try to hold on: he may just grow up to write a Gospel!

**Joseph.** Joseph knew that he should not betray his master, nor commit adultery. He was a vigorous young man, and Mrs. P. was beautiful, but he said "No." Nancy Reagan's "Just say no!" may be a simplistic prescription for an immensely complex problem. But "no" is still one of the most important words for Christians — one that we un-learn at our own peril. Our children need to hear it from us. Our friends who tempt us with drinks, drugs, or shady deals need to hear it from us. And our political leaders need to hear it from us — often.

**John the Baptist.** Reversing the usual treatment which focuses on Jesus' fulfilling of John's ministry, explore John's contribution to Jesus' ministry. John contributed to Jesus' intellectual maturity by his prophetic preaching. He contributed to Jesus' spiritual maturity by baptizing him. And he contributed to Jesus' emotional maturity by giving him a chance to learn how to handle a rival, with love.

**Barabbas.** The Zealot on Death Row illustrates several perennial features of the human tragic-comedy: the frustration of the little fellow in the face of entrenched big power; the popularity and ultimate futility of violence; the influence of politics on the administration of justice. But the most striking thing about Barabbas is that he was the first man who could say, "Jesus died for me," and be correct not just spiritually but literally.

**Jacob.** He was a rogue and a scrapper and a survival artist, but he longed for God, and God did have a plan for him. However, Jacob could not hoist himself one inch nearer God until God let down that ladder for him. The ladder is God's: a symbol of God's descent to us, God's gracious condescension fulfilled once and for all in the Incarnation.

# Part Two

*Sermons*

# 1. Thomas The Doubter

## *Introductory Note*

"Thomas the Doubter" is obviously an Easter sermon. However, for Christians every Lord's Day is Easter, because ours is a Resurrection faith. Without the Resurrection, we have nothing distinctive — for our own comfort and growth or for a world in pain.

In "Thomas the Doubter" I hazard a hypothesis about Thomas' life prior to his meeting Jesus. The hypothesis seems fairly plausible. His nickname, Didymus, appears in the biblical record (John 11:16).

"Thomas the Doubter" argues for the value of honest doubt as an integral part of authentic Christian faith. In an age of dizzying change and awesome uncertainty, the sellers of closed systems with cut-and-dried answers are getting rich. We need not, we cannot afford to, envy them.

---

## *Scripture: John 20:19-29*

A brilliant young lawyer I knew years ago quit his career, even though married and the father of several children, in order to enter the Christian ministry. When asked what moved him to make such an unconventional, high-risk decision, he wrote: "It is true that most pagans I know are quite honestly not concerned about death. But even in an affluent society, the death rate is still 100 percent — and few people die laughing...."

What do you make of Job's question (14:14), "If a man die, shall he live again?" Or of our Lord's response (John 14:19), "Because I live, you also shall live"? Of course, as long as death seems far away, we are quite unconcerned. While we are young and/or in good health, death holds no personal reality for us unless we happen to be living in a war zone. But, at just one remove, death is likely to be quite real to us at any age. Right now someone who means much to you may be walking in death's shadow. Or perhaps someone very close to you has just died, robbing you of a cherished, taken-for-granted presence, leaving you baffled, resentful, frightened.

Yes, it is hard to be an Easter Christian, a Resurrection Christian, all year round. The closer the threat, the greater the fear, the harder it is to hold on to the Easter faith and the more inclined we are to sympathize with Thomas the Doubter.

## Doubting Thomas

At first glance, Thomas does not cut a very good figure. The first three Gospels merely list his name among the Twelve. The Gospel of John has more to say about him, but nothing particularly flattering.

Thomas is first shown at a conference of the disciples in the province of Perea where they have taken refuge after the first threat of hostility from the authorities in Jerusalem. Suddenly a messenger comes to tell Jesus that his friend, Lazarus of Bethany, the brother of Martha and Mary, is dying. Jesus is ready to start out for Bethany at once, but the Disciples resist him. "Master," they plead, "the people were but now seeking to stone you, and are you going there again?" But when they cannot persuade him, they yield. Only Thomas takes the dark view. "Let us also go," he says, "that we may die with him."

The second time Thomas says something for the record is at the Last Supper. Having long since accepted the worst, Thomas appears grieved and peeved at the Master's attempt to comfort him. Jesus is talking about his Father's house with many rooms where he is about to go in order to prepare a place for his friends. Assuming that the Disciples understand, Jesus says, "You know where I am going, and you know the way." But Thomas interrupts, "Lord, we do not know where you are going. How can we know the way?" The poetry of Jesus seems wasted on Thomas. Thomas wants prose — plain, literal prose.

So far Thomas has revealed himself as a kind of Stoic: looking for the worst, finding it, and bravely facing it. At the next stage, however, his desperate courage becomes sheer despair, just one step removed from blasphemy. Having missed the evidence of the Resurrection which his fellow disciples have experienced in his absence, Thomas rejects their testimony vehemently: "Unless I see in his hands the print of the nails, and place my finger in the mark of the nails, and place my hand in his side, I will not believe!" There he is, Thomas the Doubter, at the bottom of bottomless despair, doubting everything except his own doubts. Behold a man who has died with Jesus but refuses to be raised with him!

## Also Called Twin

How can we excuse such un-apostolic behavior? I believe that our responsibility is not to excuse at all but to try to understand. I have a hypothesis — farfetched perhaps but not lacking in plausibility. Thomas was nicknamed DIDYMUS which is Greek for TWIN; in fact, the name "Thomas" is a transliteration of the Aramaic word for twin. Question: what happened to the other twin?

In the absence of any clue in the New Testament, I feel free to suggest that Thomas had a twin brother who died, in the full flower of youth, just before Thomas met Jesus. That is my hypothesis. Now let me develop it a little further.

Suppose that this twin brother had been very close to Thomas, that he was half of Thomas' life, and that his death left Thomas a mere survivor, with no life of his own — and that Thomas continued in this state, hollow with grief, empty of feeling, until he met Jesus.

Imperceptibly, almost in spite of himself, Thomas found himself being reawakened to life by the Master, transferring his grief-stricken love from his dead brother to Jesus. The Master, whom his friends came to know as "a friend who sticks closer than a brother," became for Thomas a Twin Brother, the One whom no one would dare take away from him.

But Thomas was a realist. Having experienced the power of death, he was unable to forget it. He knew that death always wins in the end. He was achingly aware of the Master's mortality, but quite deaf to the music of his promises.

Thus, when the others were ready to take Jesus at his word with the relative unconcern of people who had never clashed with death head-on and been left bruised and bleeding, Thomas showed a more perceptive, a more heroic courage. "Let us also go," he said, "that we may die with him" (John 11:16). Thomas was ready to die with Jesus, because he would not live without him. Having half-died in the death of his beloved twin brother, he did not wish to outlive the One who had more than taken his brother's place.

But Jesus kept turning the knife in Thomas' wound. Jesus insisted on repeating the promise which, Thomas knew, no mortal could fulfill. In fact, it seemed cruel even to make such a promise within the hearing of one who so well knew the awful finality of death. "Lord," Thomas burst forth at the Last Supper, "we do not know where you are going: how can we know the way?" (John 14:5). But what Thomas really meant to say was: "Lord, I know where you are going. You are going to your death, and I want to go with you. So please, do what you must, but stop consoling us when you know that there is no consolation."

## One Of The Twelve

I am certain that the apostles were provoked with Thomas. They resented his throwing cold water on their confidence in Jesus or, rather, on that "all will be well" attitude into which their dependent, immature faith so easily degenerated. They regarded Thomas' question at the Last Supper as uninspired and ill-timed.

Nor were they particularly surprised when Thomas did not join them after the Crucifixion. They could not blame him for having deserted Jesus: that they had all done. Ironically, Judas was the only one who had the courage and the required self-loathing to follow Jesus into death. As for Thomas, he might be somewhere, anywhere, contemplating the same tragic course. He had never been a gracious companion to the others. It was not surprising that he should not be seeking their company now.

Then Jesus appeared to the apostles — just a few hours after his first appearance to Mary Magdalene. Ten were present to witness the impossible. Ten testified to the miracle of the Master's victory over death. Did they go looking for Thomas to tell him the news? Or did they wait until, led by some instinct, by some stubborn hope lodged deep below the surface of consciousness, Thomas groped his way back into that Upper Room — to find there a circle of light and a chorus of praise?

We do not know. All we do know is that, with his accustomed honesty, courage, and despair, Thomas rejected their witness. His crude words must have hurt him more than they hurt the others. For them, they were only blasphemy. For Thomas, they were a creed: the creed of a mortal man trapped in his mortality, the creed of a twice-dead man whose only hope was that death would soon try for the third time and bring him at last the end of grief and the release of oblivion.

That was all anyone could hope for before that first Easter Day. Thomas was only more forthright in his recognition of the fact of death, more uncompromising with wishful thinking, more proudly wedded to his own integrity in the face of death. The other ten had the easy part now. They had seen the dawn which Thomas had not seen. It ill behooved them to be impatient with Thomas.

## An Apostle Of Jesus Christ

But Jesus was not impatient. Jesus had not forgotten that Thomas had been the only one who wanted to go with him to the side of Lazarus, not because he thought that all would be well but because he knew that nothing would be well. Nor had Jesus rebuffed Thomas for questioning him about his destiny. Instead, he had responded with one of the greatest summaries of Christian faith: "I am the Way, the Truth, and the Life" (John 14:6). No, Jesus never lost patience with Thomas, because Jesus values honest doubt more than he values blind belief.

For belief can be blind. Gullibility, superstition, and prejudice are all close kin to belief. The lazy acceptance of outworn theories wrongly enthroned as dogmas has lent respectability to man's inhumanity to man, retarded the progress of human betterment, kept the human spirit in a prolonged, unlovely infancy. But to every generation God grants a few men and women who will not believe

41

just because it is the thing to do: men and women who will question and probe and search.

Thomas would not believe on anyone's say-so, even Jesus', but he was capable of faith. For faith is personal trust, with unflinching honesty, and courage to accept not only the best but the worst. Thomas did not really want to test the Risen Lord, crudely and literally. Thomas wanted to believe in the Resurrection more than anyone. But he wanted Jesus to welcome investigation.

There is hardly anything more foolish and self-defeating than to try to "protect" Jesus, or the Bible, from the scrutiny of open-minded seekers or even from the irreverent prying of scoffers. Seekers will always find more than they have come for. Scoffers will often stop scoffing and start thinking. Only the uncritical, anxiously protective, and egotistically possessive "believers" stand to lose anything at all. They stand to lose their little dogmas and puny self-respect, while the Risen Lord shows Doubting Thomas his wounded hands and side, and Thomas sinks to his knees whispering, "My Lord and my God!"

Thus Thomas the Doubter becomes Thomas the Apostle not in spite of his doubts but thanks to his doubts. Far from rejecting him, Jesus grants him the extraordinary honor of a special appearance. Jesus knew how badly the Church needed Thomas. He knew that a converted skeptic is uniquely qualified to convert skeptics.

The mind of "mass man" is always for sale. The mind of a man or woman who insists on being an individual, in all the awful loneliness of individuality, is not for sale at all. This is the person Jesus wants the most: the scholar or scientist who will pursue truth wherever it may lead; the citizen of the world who accepts all human beings as sisters and brothers in utter disregard of national, racial, or class labels; the true "humanist" whose curiosity and compassion encompass everything human, but who also hungers and thirsts for meaning beyond this brittle life....

Have you lost a twin — someone in whose death half of you seems dead? Are you afraid of death — for someone you love, or for yourself? Are you unable or unwilling to be comforted by springtime, romanticized "immortality," and the expensive trickery of the undertaker's magic? Then take Thomas. Take the Doubter who went all the way, and rest your faith in his faith. Take that kneeling figure surrounded by the radiance of the Risen Lord. Say with him: "My Lord and my God!" Then hear with him the tender, final Beatitude uttered by our Lord: "Blessed are those who have not seen, and yet believe...."

# 2. Jonah

## Introductory Note

This treatment of the Book of Jonah takes the story virtually at face value though admitting the obvious: that it is not history but a parable. The accent here is on Jonah, the man, a human being very much like us whose quarrel with God, while unfolding within a fanciful and politically loaded story, resembles our ongoing quarrel with God who steadfastly refuses to act as we feel God should or wish God would.

I have tried to treat Jonah without condescension, with sympathy and humor, including such humorous anachronisms as placing him on a hill outside Nineveh, with his Geiger counter handy, waiting for God to "nuke" the hated city.

My main goal, however, has been to relate the story to our "faith journey" in order to show how, at any stage of our quarrel with God, we are dependent on God's amazing grace embodied and made effective for us by Jesus, the crucified and risen Lord.

---

## Scripture: Jonah 1, 3, 4

The story of Jonah is remembered chiefly for Jonah's trip in the belly of that big fish, which was not a whale because a whale is not a fish. There really was a Jonah, son of Amittai. He prophesied in Israel in the eighth century, B.C., and what little we know about him we can find in 2 Kings 14:25. But, except for borrowing his name, the Book of Jonah, which is really a story about a prophet named Jonah, has nothing to do with the eighth century prophet.

The story about this Jonah, written by an unknown author, was written well after the Babylonian Exile, sometime during the fifth

45

century B.C., and it voices an inspired protest against narrow-hearted nationalism while it pleads for reconciliation even with the nation's most cruel enemies

That is the well-known main theme of the Book of Jonah. But the Word of God in this little book is not confined to the main theme. The Word is present also in the personality of Jonah, in his character and actions, in *his quarrel* with God. The writer presents the quarrel in three stages.

### Disobedience

The first stage we may call Jonah's disobedience to God.

Out of a clear sky, God sends Jonah on a repulsive mission. He commands Jonah to go to Nineveh, the capital of Assyria, the current overlord and oppressor of his people, to preach to the hated Assyrians so that they may have a chance to repent and be spared the awful judgment which God has in store for them.

It is difficult for us to conceive how monstrous this mission must have appeared to Jonah. During the two centuries when the Assyrians lorded it over them, the Jews came to hate them as bitterly as they had every right to hate Hitler's Germans. Any notion of forgiveness or reconciliation would understandably appear as absurd, indeed treasonable. Nothing short of the destruction of Nineveh, the obliteration of Assyria, could really satisfy a pious and patriotic Hebrew like Jonah!

But God was not thinking like a pious and patriotic Hebrew. God was divinely unorthodox in his thinking about the Assyrians and their sinful capital. God remembered that, as cruel as the Assyrians had been not only to the Jews but to all their subject peoples, they were still members of the human race, children of the Heavenly Father.

But, unlike God, Jonah could not conceive of forgiving the Assyrians. To do so would have deprived him and his fellow Jews of their most trusted and efficient scapegoat. For whatever was wrong with Jonah personally or with his people, there were always the Assyrians to blame and to hate. How could anyone be expected to give up such a priceless emotional prop?

46

So, instead of taking the first caravan to Nineveh, Jonah took the first ship going west, to Tarshish. The Jews were a nation of landlubbers. Anyone putting an ocean between himself and God was getting as far away from God as was humanly possible!

But in Jonah's case, according to our story, it was not far enough. God stowed away on Jonah's ship. God always stows away in our conscience, whenever we are trying to run and hide. There is no alibi God cannot spot, no hiding place God cannot find, no bluff God cannot call. God found Adam in the shrubbery. God found Jonah in the ship's hold. And God finds us, every time, behind our plain or fancy excuses.

Jonah did not get away with it. The Lord appointed a great storm to rock the ship in which Jonah was trying to rock his conscience to sleep. It took terror, raw terror, to bring Jonah to his senses. He had been very successful in keeping up a good front, until the storm broke. Then he cracked. The flashes of lightning revealed a man in terror for his life, a man riddled with guilt, a man whose disobedience to God had involved a whole shipload of innocent, unsuspecting people in raging disaster.

But Jonah was still a potential prophet. God's choice of him had not been a mistake. In anguish and penitence he pleaded with the captain, "Take me up and throw me into the sea ... for I know it is because of me that this great tempest has come upon you!"

## Disapproval

Now Jonah's quarrel with God moves to its second stage: Jonah's disapproval of God.

At first, everything seems fine. Jonah has been reappointed to go to Nineveh, and he has obeyed. He enters Nineveh and sets up his portable pulpit about one-third of the way to downtown. He is going to be a dutiful and conscientious prophet. He is also going to show God how foolish and unrealistic it is to expect a change of heart of these barbarians! In fact, God will soon admit that Jonah was right, and then God will send pestilence and fire upon Nineveh at once. A delightful prospect for a pious and patriotic Hebrew like Jonah!

But something goes wrong. Jonah has hardly reached the first point of his sermon when the people of Nineveh begin to respond. First two or three, then dozens, then hundreds. The news spreads — through the industrial suburbs to the business district, through the business district to the residential suburbs, not skipping the campus of the University of Nineveh, nor its many temples. A miracle is happening: in a matter of just a few hours, the king himself, in sackcloth and ashes, proclaims a national fast, the redress of all social injustice, and official public repentance! Never was a sermon more unexpectedly, more spectacularly effective! Never was a preacher more dumbfounded — and angry!

Angry? Yes, mortally angry! Why? Because God had dared to act differently from what Jonah expected, from the way Jonah thought God should act! Whenever we remind ourselves, complacently, that God made us in his image, we should also remind ourselves that we keep remaking God in our image. The biblical word for this activity is idolatry: the worship of anyone or anything other than, or less than, the God of Abraham, Isaac, and Jacob, the God and Father of Jesus of Nazareth!

Whenever I overhear teenagers criticizing their parents, I wonder how well they would do if they were given a chance to trade places with them. Whenever I hear a man say, "Now if I were running this country," I would wish I could let him try, just for a day. And whenever I realize that I am inwardly "playing God," questioning God's competence, disapproving God's action or lack of action, I try to imagine what a mess I would make if I had to govern the universe.

It helps to keep in mind that "universe" means "one verse." All we know, all we can know, is just one stanza of the endless, cosmic song about the power of God and the wisdom of God. And while all is not right with the world, far from it, the Scriptures proclaim with a single voice: God is on the job, in firm control of you and me, accountable to neither you nor me!

## Disappointment
The last stage of Jonah's quarrel with God we may call Jonah's disappointment in God.

When Jonah realized that the Assyrians were really repenting and that God had promised to forgive and spare them if they did, he still could not quite believe it. It is always difficult to believe that God will not personally and spectacularly avenge us on anyone who has ever done us wrong. If God does not send the plague on our enemies, how about dropping at least a small nuclear bomb on their heads?

So Jonah leaves the city and settles on a hilltop just outside Nineveh, at a safe distance. He puts on his goggles, keeps his Geiger counter handy, and waits hopefully for the show. It is hot, very hot. The hours pass at a crawl. Nothing happens. Then, suddenly, Jonah feels deliciously cool. While he was dozing, God had raised a vegetable sunshade over his head, for his comfort. Jonah is delighted. More than ever he feels sure that he is being the object of God's special care. Now, at any moment, God will delight him by blowing Nineveh sky high!

But God does not oblige. Instead, God appoints a worm to sabotage Jonah's sunshade. When the sun rises the next morning, it beats down on Jonah's skull with tropical cruelty, and once again Jonah is ready to give up. What kind of God is God, anyway? Does God not owe it to Jonah, a prophet, to keep him alive — and comfortable? Is Jonah not a privileged man, son of a privileged race, adherent of a privileged religion? Jonah is angry, but this time it is the anger, the galling anger of deep disappointment in God.

But Jonah was doomed to be disappointed in God, and so are we if we insist that God must arrange everything to suit us as long as we have done our part by obeying God's commands. Oh, we may not throw a tantrum when a favorite ball game is cancelled because of rain. "It's good for the farmers," we say and half mean it. But when our business is wiped out in what seems to be a series of bad breaks, we are not likely to take it as well. We find others to blame — our associates, our competitors, the government — but deep down we are really blaming God. "Why did this happen to me?" we lament. "How could God let it happen? To me?" When illness strikes, or sorrow, or any kind of serious loss, we first look for someone else to blame, to serve as scapegoat. Next we blame

God. The last thing we are likely to do is to blame ourselves, even a little bit....

So the story of Jonah ends, inconclusively, with God's concern for the poor sheep and cows of Nineveh, because God's mercy never ends, and because our quarrel with God also goes on, endlessly, as long as we persist in our disobedience, our disapproval, our disappointment.

But the quarrel does not have to go on forever. God would put a stop to it today, in your life and mine. God has taken action to stop the quarrel. The action occurred nearly two thousand years ago, but it can take effect in our life any day, even today.

We are trying to run away from God, from whatever God is plainly commanding us, through our conscience. But there was "One who was obedient unto death, even death on a cross."

We fret and rebel because God does not make every wish of ours come true. But there was One who taught us to pray, "not my will but thine be done."

We are fickle in our loyalty to God, grandly accepting and expecting God's blessings but breaking faith with God at the first sign of adversity. But there was One who did not cry out, "My God, my God, why hast thou forsaken me?" until the rushing of his blood was like the thunder of cannon in his ears: and even then it was not his last word, because he would give up his life with a triumphant cry of trust: "Father, into Thy hands I commit my spirit!"

This is the One who brought to light, and to life, what we know as the gospel, the Good News, which the writer of the Book of Jonah could not even glimpse. This is the One whose matchless life and redeeming death are available to you and to me.... Amen.

# 3. Martha

## Introductory Note

This treatment of Martha is different from the usual in at least two respects. Instead of belittling her for her misplaced priorities, we spend most of our time finding out how much like her we are. Instead of leaving her as recipient of Jesus' rebuke, no matter how affectionate, we are reminded that she did heed the Master's words, that she did change, which gives us hope that we, too, can change.

The message is designed primarily for the active ten percent or maximum one-third of a suburban Protestant church, but it is just as likely to apply to the activist, workhorse segment of any American congregation, because activism is the hallmark of American church life, regardless of doctrine or ritual.

I believe that wrapping the message around the character of Martha makes it more interesting and memorable as well as a great deal less preachy while validating the sermon as a sermon — over against the self-help magazine article it might have been.

---

## Scripture: Luke 10:38-42; John 11:17-22

In a village between Jerusalem and Jericho, named Bethany, lived two sisters and their brother. Their home had become our Lord's favored place of rest, his home away from home after his own family had more or less given up on him. With Martha and Mary and Lazarus, Jesus and the disciples were able to relax and to renew their strength for the work they had to do in the countryside and, eventually, in Jerusalem.

In spite of the Master's gentle rebuke to Martha recorded in the tenth chapter of Luke's Gospel, we remember her with sympathy, indeed with a feeling of deep kinship, because Martha is one of us: responsible, busy, frequently overwhelmed.

Christians are, for the most part, extremely responsible people. In a nation where at any time millions are in full, headlong flight from responsibility, this is a sincere compliment: to Martha and to most of us who find it easy sympathetically to identify with her.

We have among us several million alcoholics who have escaped from responsibility — into a tragic prison of their own making. We are aware, more dimly but with far greater distaste and fear, of hundreds of thousands of drug addicts in similar flight. And we all wonder from time to time how many of our tens of thousands of highway deaths are really accidental. Unconscious desire to get away from it all is likely to play a large part in many of them. The coroner's verdict may read "accident." But I believe that the Coroner employed by God's Supreme Court changes many of these verdicts to "suicide" or "murder."

But we, well-churched Christians, are not trying to escape from responsibility! On the contrary: we are usually the people with ideals, with get-up-and-go, with challenges clearly perceived and squarely met. Is it not strange, then, how often we feel like shouting, "Help! I am snowed under!"?

Of course, no one intends to disparage your willingness to assume responsibility in any good cause in the community, let alone in the church. Service is the very watchword of the Christian life. Service beyond the line of duty has been the hallmark of Christians throughout the centuries. There is always so much more good work than there are workers to do it! Any leader of any organization working for human betterment, religious or secular, will surely say a loud "Amen!" to our Lord's wistful exclamation: "The harvest, indeed, is plentiful, but laborers are few!"

In a typical church, ten percent of the members do just about all the work. In the major political parties, the figure is two percent or less. But across the board, church people take on more volunteer work, both church and community work, than do their unchurched fellow-citizens. The record of service is impressive, but the cry, "Help! I am snowed under!" resounds with disturbing frequency in Christian homes and in the offices of pastors and other counseling professionals.

So there is something a little worrisome about our good works. There seems to be a flight *into* responsibility just as there is a flight *from* responsibility. Just as some of us flee into drink or drugs, others flee into an excessive and self-defeating array of otherwise useful and admirable good works.

## Danger Signals

Of course, all good works are not the result of flight. Many people, especially Christians, serve for the joy of serving, as a means of thanksgiving to God, as an expression of love for their fellow humans. It would be absurd as well as unfair to suggest that all the energy expended in voluntary service, in the church or elsewhere, is merely a socially acceptable way to act out a death wish! On the other hand, it would be foolish to ignore the many danger signals which are blinking for us — and for all highly organized, highly competitive, highly responsible persons. We dare not pretend that our Lord's description of Martha as "distracted by much serving" might not also apply to a great many of us.

What are some of these danger signals?

One starts to blink when any one of our service projects turns into a chore. When you begin to wish, shamefacedly, that you did not have to do what you committed yourself to doing, look out! Any good work performed in the spirit of a chore, even if it is tending crippled children, loses not only its zest but much of its actual usefulness.

Another signal starts blinking when you begin to resent the relative inactivity of others in comparison with your own feverish activity, when you are quick to say, with Martha, "Lord, do you not care that my sister has left me to serve alone?" Such irritation, no matter how objectively legitimate, is a symptom of battle fatigue.

But the clearest danger signal is the old song, "I'm just a girl (or boy) who can't say no," on your Christian lips. When just any call to service strikes you with irresistible force, look out! You now have a full-blown "Martha complex"! Martha was "anxious and troubled about many things." I am sure they were all good

53

things, like cooking for Jesus and the disciples, just as all the things you have taken on are surely good things, deserving of responsible concern, participation, leadership. But when we just "can't say no," we are likely to be in full flight from something.

## What Are We Running From?

Suppose that the shoe fits, that some of us are actually daughters and sons of Martha, full of good works but tired, anxious, compulsive. And suppose that we are in effect keeping ourselves so busy because we are running away from something. What may that something be?

Without meaning to play Sigmund Freud or trying to sell self-analysis kits, a few possible reasons do come to mind.

For example, we may be snowed under with good works because, unadmittedly, we are afraid to be alone. For when we are alone, ultimate and threatening questions float to the surface of our consciousness. Why this second-rate existence when we were sure that ours would be a first-rate life? Are my children really exceptional or are they just average and, if so, am I riding them too hard to succeed? Is it really possible that I am not immortal? Oh, it is so much easier to organize and improve the lives of our young people, our minorities, our elderly by working on committees or in groups. Group thinking is safe thinking. Group talk is guarded by hundreds of protective conventions which prevent us from "getting personal." By unspoken, common consent we ignore those huge, rock-hard questions that frighten us. So we go out again to a meeting, a party, a fundraiser.

There may be a different reason, too. We may be immersing ourselves in good works in order to avoid *one* good work, one challenge which lies, gauntlet-like, at our feet, but which we have been afraid to pick up. The good things we do may be the safer, easier options. It is safer, easier to send or even carry charity baskets to the poor than to confront our friends, our bosses, our husbands or wives who, in the name of sound business practice or practical politics, are keeping the poor poor. It is safer, easier, to write a letter to the President than to march shoulder to shoulder with long-haired young men and thin-lipped girls in jeans carrying placards, while our friends look away in embarrassment and the people on the sidelines hoot and jeer. But it may be just such a seemingly "far-out" action God has laid on our conscience, so that now we plead: "Look here, Lord: what you are asking of me is not really my speed. Furthermore, I am much too busy; in fact, I am working my head off doing all these other things!"

There may also be a third reason, except that it deserves to move to first place. Is it possible, just barely possible, that some of us well-churched Christians may be trying to flee from God — into that overload of responsibilities which then brings forth that "Help! I am snowed under!" cry? An annoying suggestion, but let us examine it anyway. Is it not true that God is most likely to confront us when we are alone? Is it not equally plausible that God will use such a moment to remind us of the gauntlet we have failed to pick up, the gauntlet at our feet, the gauntlet with our name on it?

Remember: Martha would not come into the living room because someone had to do the cooking. But is it not possible that Martha kept herself extra busy that day deliberately to avoid Jesus, lest the Master say something to her, something she really longed to hear but was afraid to hear? Something that would challenge her more deeply than all her dutiful good works? Something that might bring her face to face with God in one shattering, healing flash? Is it not possible that Martha begrudged Mary her conversation with Jesus, because she was frightened of what a few words with Jesus, a few personal words, might do to her? Or for her?

## Can We Stop Running?

Jesus said to Martha, "Few things are needful." Four short words, but how threatening to our value system, our frantically hyped prosperity, our whole American way of life! Not more gadgets but fewer. Not bigger cars but smaller ones and perhaps, heresy of heresies, no car at all. Not multiplication but simplification. Not competition but cooperation. To be content with less rather than condemned to more. Might *this* be the alternative to our "distracted serving," this the brake to slow our headlong flight, this the discipline by which to lose this whole phony world and gain our soul?

"Few things are needful," Jesus said to Martha, "or only one thing." No, Jesus did not prescribe a life of mystic idleness or idle mysticism, a life of all words and no action. He did not suggest that no one should be cooking dinner or that Mary should never be expected to help Martha in the kitchen. He did suggest, I am certain, that Martha should not bother to put on five-course meals all the time — that two or three courses or even a savory casserole might do just as well — and that she should take time to be with him rather than just feed him, to *be* rather than always *do*....

Unless we take time out just to *be*, especially to be *with the Lord*, in reflection and prayer, the pressures upon us will overwhelm us, especially if we are sons and daughters of Martha, ultra-responsible Christians. Good works can become a joyless treadmill. Cooking for everyone, like Martha, on eight burners, will soon have us looking for a stove with sixteen, and running, running, running, without ever asking ourselves why we are running or what we are running from. But if we stop long enough to hear the Master's gentle rebuke, we may be able to glimpse, perhaps for the first time, the *life of faith* beyond this life of work, work, work.

Like Jesus' own life, it will not be an idle life. Far from it. But it will be, like Jesus' own life, a life balanced on the fathomless tide of God's mercy and love. A life of self-giving activity alternating with prayer, meditation, and guilt-free leisure. A life of fewer responsibilities more effectively carried out. A life of greater challenges more bravely faced.

Yes, for all of us who claim his name, Jesus proposes, and enables, *a life with time to spare*. Time to let the taste of both joy and sorrow linger a while. Time to give to others not just things but ourselves. Time to think, even about death, serenely and without dread....

If we learned about Martha only from Luke's Gospel, we could not be sure that she really heard the Master's words. But there is that story in John's Gospel, about the death of her brother, Lazarus, where Martha — not Mary but Martha — is revealed as possessing the more mature faith. It is Martha, the liberated drudge, who says to Jesus, "Lord, if you had been there, my brother would not have died. But even now I know that, whatever you ask of God, God will give you."

This Martha did not learn in the kitchen.... Amen.

# 4. Daniel And His Friends

## *Introductory Note*

Preaching on Daniel and his three friends enables us to take our hearers on a lovely walk down Nostalgia Lane, because this is one story they surely remember from Sunday School days. As a children's story, the story fairly tells itself.

But the story also reminds us that God will not necessarily perform a miraculous rescue for us just because we have been righteous and brave. And to suggest that God may not be counted on to keep us cool and safe in the "burning fiery furnace," in Babylon or in Auschwitz, is likely to be, is meant to be, a disturbing thought.

Thus the children's story, with its delightful humor and Disneyesque imagery, suddenly rises to its proper "R" rating.

---

## *Scripture: Daniel 1:1-21; 3:1-18*

Nebuchadnezzar, king of Babylonia, had a troublesome minority on his hands. The Jews were stubborn. They refused to be melted into Babylon's melting pot. They clung, stubbornly, to their language, their customs, their religion.

Like any smart tyrant, Nebuchadnezzar knew that his hope lay with the youth. Old people were not worth the bother. People in their prime might offer too much resistance. Children and young people were the key. "Who has the youth, has the future."

Nebuchadnezzar knew young people well. He did not waste time and money trying to win over all the Jewish boys in Babylon. He took the leaders, "youths without blemish, handsome, and skillful in all wisdom." He took the honor roll students who were also top athletes. He knew that if you got them on your side, all the other young Jews would follow like sheep — or goats.

59

By Nebuchadnezzar's decision, Daniel and his friends found themselves suddenly a minority within a minority. They were Jews in Babylon. They were also being singled out for special treatment. The king had decided to forgive them for being Jews and to grant them all the advantages available to members of Babylon's nobility. They were to live at the royal court, have all their needs supplied, be treated like princes. They were going to have silver spoons stuck in their mouths — and pushed down their throats.

For Nebuchadnezzar's generosity had a purpose. By becoming page boys in the royal court, Daniel and his friends were not only to remain in the king's service all their life: they were also going to provide for their fellow Jews a shining example of the wisdom of the proverb: "When in Babylon, it pays to do as the Babylonians do."

Nebuchadnezzar was not going to miss a single trick in educating Daniel and his friends into Babylonian conformity.

They were to be given new names, not just because their Jewish names were hard for Babylonians to pronounce but because, in biblical times, a new name signified a new life. That is why Abram changed his name to Abraham. That is why Saul switched to his Roman name Paul. Daniel and his friends were expected to surrender their Jewish identity with their Jewish names. The faith of their fathers was going to perish with the names which their fathers had given them.

Daniel and his friends were also going to receive a first-class Babylonian education. Nebuchadnezzar instructed the keeper of the royal harem, who was also responsible for the training of page boys in the royal court, that these four young Jews should be taught "the letters and language of the Chaldeans." The Chaldeans were the ruling class of the realm. They were also specialists in magic, astrology, and other prestigious sciences. Clearly, Daniel and his friends were headed for the Ivy League.

As for the inner man, Nebuchadnezzar ruled that the four young Jews should receive the same food he ate and the same wines he drank. The royal cuisine was rich and spicy. Daniel and his friends were young, healthy men who loved food and would surely not object to getting the finest quality as long as they were getting enough!

Thus everything was looking up from Nebuchadnezzar's point of view. But from the point of view of Daniel and his friends, things looked grim. They were Jews, heirs of the Jewish faith, members of the Jewish religious community. Their moral and religious commitments forbade them to melt into Babylon's melting pot.

They had their own integrity to consider, of course. The king's plan would have put them to an agonizing test, even if there had been no one else to consider. But there is always someone else to consider. Integrity is never our private property. It always belongs to our public: to all the people, known or unknown to us, who look to us for an example, for leadership.

In Daniel's case, he and his friends had actually been selected for their publicity value. If they could be assimilated unprotestingly, if they could be bribed into shedding their Jewish religion and their Jewish moral values, their school chums and playmates would follow. So would some members of their families. Before long, only die-hards would hold on to their Jewish identity. Eventually, the die-hards would die out, and Nebuchadnezzar's experiment, a pioneer experiment in education for conformity, would have succeeded without using such crude methods as Hitler would use 2,500 years later to get rid of the Jews.

At the outset, Daniel and his friends were neither rebels nor heroes. They were quite willing to go along with the king's plan, up to a point. They liked the idea of getting a first-class education, with full scholarships. They did not really mind those tongue-twisting Babylonian names. They thought: "As long as we know who we are, what does it matter what they call us?" They were ready to submit to Nebuchadnezzar's "generosity" and to learn, at his expense, how to beat the Babylonians at some of their own games.

But this business of diet nearly finished them before they had a chance to get started. For one thing, being healthy and tough, they despised the fancy cuisine of the royal court. They gagged on the gooey sundaes they were being served, not even in mid-afternoon but for breakfast! They knew that overindulgence in rich food and drink made people soft, not only physically but mentally and

61

spiritually. They also knew that this was more than a matter of diet — that it was a matter of religion. Breaking the diet prescribed by Moses amounted to compromise in the Jewish community, and compromise, especially in captivity, amounted to treason.

Daniel and his friends were rigid about their religion. Rigid people may not be much fun. The leading Puritans were not much fun, but they were brave and rugged people, and they laid a solid foundation for our country. They knew, as did the four young Jews in our story, that there are things in life that are more important and of more lasting value than popularity and security.

As Christians, we are supposed to have a faith that shows. Even those who openly belittle or deny the Christian faith, expect us to stand up and to speak up for what we profess. They may try to shout us down. They may succeed in beating us down. But they will be genuinely disappointed, as well as confirmed in their contempt for Christianity, if we do not show our faith.

Daniel and his friends let their faith show, literally. They persuaded the king's chef to put them to a ten-day test in order to compare the effect of their frugal, kosher diet with the effect of the over-rich diet fed to the Babylonian young men. At the end of the ten days, the chef was convinced. The faces of the young Babylonians were flabby and full of pimples. The faces of the young Jews were firm and smooth.

Of course, from a scientific point of view, this is hardly more than a fable. But the moral and spiritual message is inescapable. Whether we are Jews or Christians, we are expected to show our faith, perhaps in our faces but surely in our actions. For the emblem of our faith is not the chameleon, that paragon of conformity. The emblem of Jewish faith is the lion, the Lion of Judah roaring for justice. And the emblem of Christian faith is the lamb, the Lamb of God who takes away the sins of the world, the non-conforming Lamb of God most powerful in his willing, purposeful, redemptive *death*!

Yes, death. For the story of Daniel and his friends is really a *children's story*, and even smart children know better than to believe such stories. Good and faithful Daniel, wearing a white hat, outwits crafty Nebuchadnezzar in the first round by gaining the right, for himself and his friends, to eat kosher in Babylon. Next thing, good and faithful Daniel refuses to worship the king's new idol. And when Nebuchadnezzar reluctantly throws him and his friends into the royal blast furnace, they come out unscathed, because that's the way it goes in children's stories if you are good and faithful.

But let's examine the story of Daniel and his friends, as *adults*. It is a story written by an unknown Jewish writer, not during the Babylonian exile, in the sixth century B.C. but sometime during the second century B.C., when the Jews were being ruled and oppressed by the Syrians. Resentment of their oppression eventually led the Jews to revolt under the leadership of a noble family, the Maccabbees. What we know as the Book of Daniel was a revolutionary tract designed to help the Maccabeean Revolution succeed, which it did.

But the story itself, as lively and well-loved as it is, raises more questions, for adults, than it answers. Does virtue really pay? Does God rescue his own in recognition of goodness and faithfulness? Will God keep it cool for his own in the royal blast furnace? Any Christian or Jew ready to answer these questions with a simple "yes" has never heard of Auschwitz. Or Majdanek. Or Treblinka. Those furnaces were not cool. They were hot. And they consumed alike the just and the unjust, the godly and the godless, with absolute impartiality.

No, these are not simple questions. They are tough questions. And the toughest of them may be whether God ever *does*, or even *can, intervene* on behalf of his own in miraculous ways. Daniel and his friends come across very positive when they claim, in the face of Nebuchadnezzar's threat, that "our God is able to deliver us from the burning fiery furnace ... " (Daniel 3:17). But some of my classmates from the Lutheran Gymnasium of Budapest, who were gassed and cremated in Auschwitz, were equally positive in their Jewish faith, perhaps to the end, when they were being marched, naked, into what they had been told were shower sheds.

Thus, if we take the faith of those young Jews in Babylon and of millions of other Jews throughout history at face value, we have a shocking problem: *God is a monster!* He knows his own. He sees their ghastly suffering. He may even be the One who has exposed them to this suffering in order to test their faith. But he *does nothing*. He lets them suffer and perish.

For anyone smart enough and brave enough to confront reality, the problem is insoluble: God cannot be *both all-powerful and all-loving*. If you insist on claiming that he is both, you will have to convince me that every one of the six million deserved to die when they did and as they did. This, in turn, would make Hitler an instrument of God's will, and his murderous madness a vehicle for God's righteousness. At which point I say, "If God is like that, you can have him — and keep him!"

Thus the story of Daniel and his friends is deeply flawed, no matter how much we like it, no matter how much we may want to believe it. But even in the most "primitive" parts of the Bible, even in the middle of simplistic, morally unacceptable materials included in this amazing library which we so lightly call "God's Word," there is always something, some little surprise, some small discordant note, which reassures us that the "Word of God" is present after all. Even in this strictly "early Hollywood" story.

Remember how the young men respond to Nebuchadnezzar's threat (Daniel 3:16-18): "O Nebuchadnezzar, our God whom we serve is able to deliver us from the burning fiery furnace, and he will deliver us out of your hand, O King. But if not, be it known to you, O King, that we will (still) not serve your gods nor worship the golden image which you have set up!" *"But if not...."* These three little words more than justify keeping the story of Daniel and his friends in the Bible!

We do not know what God is or is not able to do. You may consider him all-powerful, if you wish. I may consider him limited or self-limited, if I prefer. What we do know is that we cannot count on God for keeping it cool for us in the furnace! Our goodness and faithfulness can never be based on any *quid pro quo*. We dare not ever say, even in a whispered prayer, "All right, God, I will be good, I will be faithful, if you will keep me safe...." God does not enter into bargains. If Daniel and his friends had been loyal and brave just because they were expecting God to keep them safe, their righteousness would have been shallow, their virtue hollow.

As Christians, we know both the power and the powerlessness of God. We celebrate the power of God on Easter Sunday — and on every Lord's Day. But the model for our life and witness is the Cross where hangs the willing Victim, utterly powerless, not rescued at the last minute nor spared a single indignity or agony; and to follow this model, God's own model for human life, in a ceaseless quest for justice and reconciliation, is meant to be *its own reward.*

If the life which Jesus has modeled for us, Cross and all, is not worth living for its own sake, it is simply not worth living. But it is! Dietrich Bonhoeffer would tell you so. Martin Luther King would tell you so. Archbishop Romero of El Salvador, gunned down in front of the altar for standing up for the poor, would tell you so. They all knew, they all lived by those three little words, "But if not...." Amen.

# 5. The Man Born Blind

## Introductory Note

Jesus lived and died a believing, practicing Jew, but he challenged and transcended the religion of his people on many points of both doctrine and practice. One of his many clashes with the Pharisees, the Ultra-Orthodox of his day, revolved around the blind beggar in John 9.

The theological problem persists, of course: how can a just God, a loving God, allow a human being to be born blind? The Pharisees' answer defends God's justice by assuming that the blindness is punishment for sin — someone's sin. Jesus' answer is no answer: it is an act of mercy. For there is no answer — except to show mercy and to keep trusting in God.

What might be no more than a clanking of theological armor is at least partly salvaged by paying attention to the man born blind as a man. At first he is a stereotype: a text for the debate. But soon he is revealed as a person with integrity, curiosity, and tenacity. Distrusted and despised as a sinner, his witness proves more than a match for the Pharisees with his shrewd mind and sharp tongue. The debate continues, but his witness must henceforth be reckoned with.

---

## Scripture: John 9:1-41

There are many things in life which make it easy for us to believe that God is love. There are memories of childhood, memories of father and mother, increasingly appreciated through the years. There are moments of tender communion between husband and wife, usually not scheduled and organized, like a birthday party,

67

but unsought and unexpected: moments in which love runs so deep that only the language of poetry or prayer can do them justice. And there are times when a baby grins at us and a little hand trustingly explores our face, and suddenly we know that God is love.

But there are other things in life which make it difficult for us to believe that God is love: not just difficult but nearly impossible. I am not thinking about man's inhumanity to man. Wars and all forms of violence are ultimately our responsibility. God is not the President of the Society for the Prevention of Cruelty to Humans. We dare not blame God for the ghastly things we do to one another or allow to be done with our approval or at least without protest.

## A Man Born Blind

But think of that man born blind, a man who has spent a lifetime in utter darkness. When you were little and your parents first pointed out to you the man with the white cane and the gentle dog, how did you react? Did you make believe for a few seconds that you were blind, too? Did you try to walk with your eyes closed? Did you keep going long enough to feel that sickening insecurity? I have always wondered whether it is more merciful to be born blind and never really to know the glory of seeing or to have something to remember, even though living in darkness. The question may be unrealistic. If there is an answer, I do not know it. But this I do know: it must be hard, brutally hard, to be blind, even in this age of Braille and radio and records and talking books and special skills to be learned and a large measure of self-esteem to be had for the effort.

It is brutally hard to be blind even today, but in Jesus' time it was infinitely harder. For one thing, there was nothing to do for a blind man except to beg. The blind man whom we meet in the ninth chapter of John's Gospel was a beggar. What else could he be? Charity in those days was literal-minded, unimaginative. It was a religious duty to give alms, and people gave, as a matter of routine, to the beggars who crowded the Temple courts. There was no recognition of the individual and his sufferings in the transaction. The giver did not become involved at all. The possibility of healing did not exist; the very concept of rehabilitation was inconceivable. Nor was there any hope in the heart of a blind man, of any blind man.

But the hardest thing for a man born blind was to know himself as an object of suspicion and reproach because of his blindness. The logic of the Pharisees and of their theology was airtight and inhuman. They interpreted congenital blindness as punishment for sin: if not the man's own sin, then surely the sin of one of his ancestors. The Pharisees remembered well the statement about God as "a jealous God, visiting the iniquity of the fathers upon the children...." They conveniently forgot the sequel where God is described as "showing steadfast love to thousands ..." (Exodus 20:5-6).

### A Case

But the disciples were also children of their time. When they became aware of the man born blind, their reaction was predictable. "Master," one of them asked Jesus, hoping to use this interesting case to resolve a continuing theological debate, "who sinned — this man or his parents — that he was born blind?" (John 9:2). The question grates on our ears, of course; but remember that, in Jesus' day, one school of rabbis argued that one could sin even in the womb!

Jesus, however, made short shrift of the question. "It was not that this man sinned or his parents," he said, "but that the works of God might be made manifest in him" (John 9:3).

Many very religious people cannot endure the notion that God is greater than they. They must have an answer for everything in terms of their own earthbound logic. They must keep convincing themselves that, for them, the mind of God is an open book. The Pharisees were of this ilk. So were the Scholastics of the Middle Ages. So are many contemporary Fundamentalist Christians who treat the Bible like a digest of laws.

But the ways of God are not necessarily logical — by our standards. It was part of Jesus' mission to reveal God's lack of logic — and excess of love. What could be more illogical than the Beatitudes? What could be more unexpected and offensive than the Son of God suspended on two wooden posts stained by his own blood

69

rather than seated in splendor on a throne of gold? But Jesus did not come to explain why God behaved this way or that way. Jesus came to reveal the love of God in action, by his perfect life and willing death. The explanations he was ready to leave to the professionals.

### A Person

The Pharisees, then, and even the disciples, saw in the man born blind a case, a human peg on which to hang a doctrine, perhaps even a doctoral dissertation. But Jesus saw the man as a person, a suffering, defeated person who was appealing to him for help. For Jesus never saw people as cases, only as persons.

Today there are doctors, not just of theology but of medicine, who forget that they are dealing with persons. The old-time family doctor did not begin to have the knowledge which even the average medical student must have nowadays in order to graduate. But the old doc did have the human touch; and, equally important, he had the time or took the time to apply it. Where many brilliant physicians today see only lungs or livers, the old doc saw persons.

Social workers and members of other helping professions are daily courting the same danger. They are so highly specialized and so hamstrung by regulations that they often fail to see the human being in the file folder. Even ministers are prone to this temptation. It is difficult to keep any perspective about ministry to persons in a success-driven, efficiency-worshiping culture. A person can get lost even in a church, especially a successful, efficient church!

### An Object Of God's Love

Jesus looked at the man born blind and saw in him a person in need, a man in whom the love of God could be made manifest and who, in turn, could make the love of God manifest to others.

These visions were both present in Jesus' mind, I am certain, but he did not make the first hinge on the second. He was going to heal this man unconditionally, even if the man never said, "Thank you," let alone became a disciple. Jesus helped and healed people without ulterior motive, to reveal God's limitless love, and from

70

time to time he earned a bonus when someone did remember to say, "Thank you," or did join his band of disciples.

With this man, Jesus was more than usually scrupulous about letting him know that there were no strings attached. He gave the man a perfect alibi. "Go, wash in the pool of Siloam," he told him (John 9:7). If he did, he could pretend that it was the water, with its alleged healing properties, that cured him. He would not have to tell anyone that Jesus even touched him. He was not running any risk at all. Jesus was giving him a foolproof chance to avoid guilt by association with him.

But this man was made of solid stuff. For one thing, he was stubbornly truthful. He had only one story and he stuck to it. He knew that it was "the man called Jesus" who had healed him. He would not use the alibi Jesus had provided for him. He would not be intimidated by either third degree or taunts. Instead, he began picking up information about "the man called Jesus." By the time the Pharisees really went to work on him, he had an interpretation. "He is a prophet," (John 9:17) the man said, which was the last thing the Pharisees wanted to hear, since they were trying to prove that Jesus was both an ordinary man and a fraud.

## A Witness To God's Love

But the man born blind was now beginning to see all sorts of things. The opening of his physical eyes was bringing him unexpected spiritual insight. He had gotten hold of just one bit of truth, but his understanding of this bit of truth grew in the process of fighting for it!

It is not necessary to know everything about Jesus. It is not even possible. The Gospel of John concludes with this lovely and completely truthful statement: "There are also other things which Jesus did; and were every one of them to be written down, the world itself could not contain the books that would be written" (John 21:25). Jesus is too big for any man's mind, but he fits readily into man's heart, because he can make a small, sluggish heart expand and throb with new life.

The man born blind did not know much about Jesus. He learned more about him by fighting for his right to witness to what he did know. He knew that he was born blind, but that now he could see. He knew that if Jesus were not a man of God, he could not have healed him. At last, when Jesus asked him point blank, "Do you believe in the Son of Man?" (John 9:35) he confessed his faith, "Lord, I believe," and he worshiped him (John 9:38).

The man born blind had come a long way. He started out with only a small fraction of the whole truth about Jesus, but that small fraction contained the essential ingredient: he knew what Jesus had done for him. Is it not true, as true as ever, that information about Jesus will take us only so far? It is helpful, indeed vital for our further growth in faith and discipleship. But it is not the main thing. The main thing, the decisive thing, is to know what Jesus has done for us. And not in the abstract, either. Nor in general, for the whole human race. Personally: for you and for me.

# 6. Adam Hiding[1]

## *Introductory Note*

We like to feel good. We like a church that makes us feel good. We like sermons that make us feel good. Many ministers have been caricatured as "Dr. Feelgood" deservedly, because they are serving up the Good News of God's love while ignoring the bad news about ourselves, about God's knowledge of us, about God's judgment on us.

This is not a "feel good" sermon. It deals with the many ways in which we try to evade responsibility for our actions or inaction. It exposes our moral nakedness in God's eyes. However, the discomfort which the sermon creates, purposefully, is mitigated and made palatable by being wrapped around the man Adam and his comically absurd attempt at hiding from God. Condemned by the "first Adam," who lives in every one of us, we are ready to hear the Good News about God's grace, revealed for our redemption in the "second Adam," our Lord Jesus Christ.

---

*Scripture: Genesis 3:1-13, 22-24*
*Psalm 139:1-12, 17-18, 22-24*

When I was a little boy, I used to play hide-and-seek with my parents. I would hide behind a chair, sticking out all over. Then I would shut my eyes and shout, "You can't see me!" And Father and Mother would oblige by calling, "Where are you?" as if they didn't know.

Adam was playing the same game with God the Father in the infancy of the human race. He had broken the only law God had imposed on him and his spouse. Now he was hiding behind some fragrant bush of Eden, with his bare bottom sticking out, pretending that God couldn't see him. And God obliged by calling, "Adam, where are you?" As if God didn't know.

### Hiding Games

It is easy to smile at the foolishness of Adam. But even Christians, who claim to be reborn through Jesus Christ, the Second Adam, continue to play the same games!

For the little bush was not the only thing behind which Adam was trying to hide from God. As soon as God yanked him out from behind the bush, Adam found another hiding-place. "The woman," he stammered, "the woman you gave me to be with, me, *she* gave me of that fruit, and I ate." Thus began man's second oldest game. The first one had been hide-and-seek. This one came to be known as passing-the-shekel. Together they are called, more elegantly, rationalization.

The fine art of rationalization is epitomized by the two great betrayals of Jesus: his betrayal by Judas and his betrayal by Pilate.

Judas, I am sure, had a rough time trying to rationalize what he was about to do. His conscience refused to cooperate. At last it came to him: he would turn the responsibility over to the constituted authorities of his nation! Jesus had frustrated him completely. Judas did not know how to deal with One who claimed — and promised — a Kingdom, but did not want to be king. Let the authorities deal with him. They would know what to do, and he, Judas, would only have done his duty as a citizen. Weren't all good Jews under orders to denounce subversives?

At the Nuremberg trials, in 1945-46, all the officials of Hitler's human slaughterhouses, from the highest to the lowest, claimed that they could not have done otherwise: they had just been carrying out orders! Having rationalized their actions by passing the buck to the authority or authorities above them, they could exterminate six million defenseless persons without losing much sleep, if any. And, so far as we can tell, few of them ever experienced anything like repentance!

But why speak of concentration camps and spectacular crimes? Who among us is without guilt? Do we not accept and carry out business policies of which our conscience disapproves? And don't we rationalize our failure to protest and our active cooperation by passing the buck to those higher up? After all, we say, it's company policy: the "management" is responsible! Oh, how easy it is to pass the buck under the heading of "company policy" or "the rules" or "the law," when we are afraid to stick our necks out! And it is true: our status, our popularity, our well-buttered bread, and sometimes even our physical safety, might be endangered if we opened our mouths on moral principle!

Pontius Pilate, and his betrayal of Jesus, represents a slightly different variety of rationalization. Pilate was also hurting, just like Judas. His conscience was giving him a hard time. So was his wife, who had a dream which confirmed his own hunch that Jesus was innocent (Matthew 27:19). And Pilate had no superior behind whom to hide — no one except the Emperor who was too far away and who couldn't be bothered, anyway. Then Pilate remembered the people, the *hoi polloi* which means, literally, "the many." And Pilate relaxed. The people would be responsible! Indeed, how could so many people making so much noise be wrong? It was all a Jewish quarrel anyway. Surely, the people knew enough to determine the guilt of one of their own! So Pilate made one more effort to appease his conscience which was still nagging him. "Whom shall I release to you, Barabbas or Jesus?" And when the *hoi polloi* yelled, "Barabbas!" voting by acclamation, Pilate, like a lowly clerk, cast the ballot for them. After carefully washing his hands.

## No Hiding Place

We try to hide from God by passing the buck to those higher up. We try to hide from God by passing the buck to the "people," the mindless majority so adept at beating into conformity, or crucifying, any creative minority. And there is a third, somewhat surprising device: we try to hide from God *in church*, in the practice of a purely formal, morally undemanding religion.

In the Book of Joshua, there is a story about a certain victory of the Hebrews which yielded them much booty. They gathered it in a central place for later, equitable distribution among themselves. However, one of their warriors named Achan knew that his share was not going to be enough to satisfy his greed. So he stole a large chunk of the loot, hid it in a safe place, and took to the woods — *no* — went to church, that is, went back to the place where his people had gathered for a service of thanksgiving! Achan knew that it would be easiest for him to escape detection in church singing hymns!

It was the same kind of rationalization — and delusion — which caused the Hebrews to build shrines for pagan gods and engage in pagan rituals outside the city limits of Jerusalem. They knew the exclusive claim of their God, YAHWEH, but they believed, for a long time, that Yahweh's jurisdiction was limited to Jerusalem so that, if they stayed far enough away from the Temple, Yahweh would not catch on to their taking part in pagan cults — especially since they were continuing to offer Yahweh the worship he desired, in the Temple! It didn't dawn on them until much later that, while Yahweh had his headquarters in the Temple, he was not a prisoner there!

What do these old stories tell us? Just this: that we, too, try hiding from God — *in prayer*, whether in church or elsewhere. How so? By assuming that God "hears" us only when we check in with an "O God," and that our closing *amen* effectively terminates the connection! So we limit our prayers to generalities, and often to trivia, on the infantile assumption that our privacy is intact whenever we do not happen to be praying with an "O God" and an "Amen" and all the rest! "The omnipresence of God means that our privacy is public" (Paul Tillich).

Many years ago I visited the Newark, New Jersey, police headquarters with the High School Fellowship of the church I was serving at the time, my very first church. In one of the rooms there was a huge table whose surface showed a map of the city of Newark. A tiny model of every patrol car in Newark was on that map somewhere; and as the patrolmen called in, the officers in charge of the map would move the little cars around to record their positions. I am sure that this tracking of patrol cars has long since been computerized, but I do believe that many of us still have this kind of a mental image of how God keeps track of us; in other words, that God does not know where we are unless we check in, through prayer; and that, without our checking in, God simply cannot find us.

But what kind of a puny God do we think God is? God knows our whereabouts at every moment. God knew where Adam was hiding. And, for all we know, the devices we use to hide from God may strike God as just as ludicrous as did Adam's bare bottom shining through the green leaves! If God is God, our life is indeed an "open book" as far as God's knowledge of what we are up to is concerned. It was this truly terrifying realization which had suddenly dawned on the writer of Psalm 139 when he burst out:

> *O Lord, Thou hast searched me and known me! Thou knowest when I sit down and when I rise up. Thou discernest my thoughts from afar. Thou searchest out my path and my lying down, and art acquainted with all my ways. Even before a word is on my tongue, O Lord, Thou knowest it altogether....*

There is, in such a sense of the presence of God, a shattering of all rationalizations, of all pious illusions and delusions, of all carefully crafted security. *God knows: We are doomed.*

### No Need To Hide

But in Christian perspective that is not the end of the story. When God called Adam out of hiding, God was calling him to judgment, to be sure. However, even while judging him, even while kicking Adam and Eve out of the Garden, God was adopting them as objects of redemptive concern. The justice of God required that Adam and Eve should forfeit the privileges of Eden. But the mercy of God prompted God to spare them and to accompany them into exile "East of Eden."

The story which the Bible tells us is, from one end to the other, a story of redemption. The sin of the First Adam sets in motion a vast scheme of redemption, which culminates in the perfect obedience, the willing sacrifice, and conclusive victory of the Second Adam — Jesus Christ.

Throughout the centuries which preceded Jesus' arrival and the fulfillment of God's saving plan, there were men and women

77

in Israel for whom the presence of God held no terror. Upon further reading, the writer of Psalm 139 proves to be one of them. He knew how terrifying God's knowledge of us can be. But he also knew, from his own experience, that there is deep joy in being known by God. "How precious are thy thoughts to me, O Lord," he wrote; "when I awake, I am still with thee." Life held no fear for this man, because his vivid awareness of God's presence in his life, by day or by night, made him feel secure. With childlike trust, he invited God to rummage around in the very depths of him:

> *Search me, O God, and know my heart!*
> *Try me, and know my thoughts!*
> *And see if there be any wicked way in me,*
> *and lead me in the way everlasting!*

Yes, the patriarchs who walked with God, the prophets who fearlessly proclaimed God's will, the nameless thousands who humbly kept God's Law — all these were mindful of their nakedness in God's sight, but they also knew that God had woven a garment of mercy around them. These men and women of ancient Israel knew that there was no place to hide from God, but they did not try to hide from God because they had experienced the comfort, the joy of God's presence, and God's everlasting mercy.

Yet none of these women and men of Old Testament times could even begin to know the length to which God would go to reclaim and save us. This knowledge was reserved for a later generation — for the people of the New Covenant, the New Testament — and it was put into undying words by Jesus himself:

> *For God so loved the world that he gave his only Son,*
> *that whoever believes in him should not perish but have*
> *eternal life. For God sent his Son into the world not to*
> *condemn the world, but that the world might be saved*
> *through him.*      — John 3:16-17

Many states in our nation have a system of annual or even semi-annual automobile inspection. Having their car inspected is something many red-blooded Americans feel pretty negative about.

Some consider it just a nuisance. Others worry about the cost of what the inspection may reveal. It takes a modicum of maturity to realize that such inspection is designed for our benefits, for our protection!

As creatures of God, we are under inspection by our Creator — not just periodically but at all times. We may fool ourselves by pretending that God cannot see us. And when we realize that God has seen us, we may further fool ourselves by trying to disclaim responsibility, to pass the buck to someone else: to a wife or a husband, a pet snake or a hated boss, a power elite or an unwashed mob.

But God's inspection of us is relentless, and we know that God is finding many awful flaws. Some of these we would like to mend, "but not just yet." Others we would like to pass off as virtues, even though we know that God's gaze cuts through our games like the proverbial hot knife through butter. What we constantly forget, stupidly forget, is that God is not "out to get us" — that God's intention is not to condemn us but to save us, even from ourselves, from the *Old Adam* who must co-exist with the *New Adam*, our rebel self with our redeemed self, until at last, by God's grace, we are born into eternal life! Amen.

---

1. Previously published in *Adam and Eve and You* (Omega Press, 1977). Copyright John R. Bodo.

# 7. The One-Talent Man

*Introductory Note*

The subtitle of this book, *Preaching On Biblical Personalities*, does not guarantee that all the persons dealt with in its pages will be historic persons. The historicity of Adam is debatable, to say the least. The hero (or antihero) of this sermon is clearly a fictitious character. He is the fall guy of Jesus' Parable of the Talents, and our Lord does not even give him a proper name. But he is a vivid biblical personality just the same. The sermon is really a rather traditional exposition and illustration of the parable, showing the world's need for one-talent men and women and stressing the responsibility of modestly endowed, average persons to put to work whatever gifts they do possess. Only in the final section does the sermon point beyond our Lord's story by citing Rosa Parks as a one-talent woman who not only did what she could but whose single gesture changed the history of race relations in our nation. Is this carrying the story of the one-talent man too far?

---

*Scripture: Matthew 25:14-30*

The Parable of the Talents climaxes in the well-known cynical saying: "To everyone who has more, more will be given ... but from everyone who has not, even what he has will be taken away." Crude? Perhaps. But true to life. In business, for example. In spite of all Chamber of Commerce folklore, you are far more likely to make it if you have a substantial bankroll at the outset — and far more likely to fail if you are under-capitalized. But making good use of what you have, no matter how little it is, can make an important difference.

81

The saying is also true with respect to our health. Mark Twain once said that every time he felt like exercising, he would lie down until the feeling passed. That is good humor but poor advice for staying fit. Whatever stamina we may have is likely to vanish if we do not exercise.

The saying makes sense also in the realm of love. Disraeli, in his later years, used to play a game with his old, ailing wife. She would ask him, "Why did you marry me?" He would reply, truthfully, "For your title and for your money." "But," Mrs. D. would resume, "if you were to do it over again...?" And Disraeli, kissing her frail hand, would answer with equal truthfulness, "Now I would marry you for love." The Disraelis did not have much going for their marriage when they were married. But by cultivating the little they had — respect, mutual usefulness, consideration — they were rewarded with a lovely, late-blooming love.

So the message of the Parable of the Talents is concerned not with how much we have at the outset, nor with how much we have to show at the end, but with how well we use whatever we have. In this perspective, the one-talent man become the reluctant hero, or anti-hero, of the story.

### The Need For One-Talent Persons

We need one-talent persons. When Lincoln quipped, "God must have loved the common people — that's why he made so many of them," he was not just being funny. There is a real need in this world for average persons who will accept themselves as they are, for what they are.

Democracy depends on the one-talent man or woman. Anybody may become President of the United States, but only one person at a time can be President. The only White House most Americans will ever inhabit is a little house with a big mortgage on it, a little old house painted white by the owner's own sticky hands. But this is not bad *per se*. A democracy of all would-be leaders soon turns into anarchy, just as an army of all would-be generals invites defeat. Democracy depends on a substantial majority of informed, participating, responsible one-talent persons.

Culture, too, depends on the one-talent man or woman. The creators, packagers, and sellers of culture in our country are very much aware of "John Q. Public," the marketplace name for the hero of Jesus' parable. John's reactions, and Jane's, are of fateful importance for the styling of our clothes, the ending of our movies, the appearance of our public buildings. One-talent Jane and John are being taken seriously! In fact, they are not being given much of a chance to rise beyond their commonness, to become more discerning, to grow up!

Religious communities also need the one-talent person. Within Christendom, appreciation for the common people, the laity (from the Greek word *laos*, "people") has been the hallmark of Protestantism from the start. Laypersons, in our belief and practice, differ from the clergy in function only: our status under God is equal. The work of God, through the Church, depends not only on the deep thinkers and the leading saints but just as much on the rank and file of faithful men and women who realize, with Paul, that "There are varieties of gifts but the same Spirit ... apportions to each one individually as he wills" (1 Corinthians 12:4-11).

Now everyone agrees with everything that has been said so far — in theory. In practice, however, the one-talent person has a rough row to hoe in a society like ours, where competition is a little tin god and money reigns supreme.

It used to be that you were somebody if you finished high school. Now you are expected to finish college and, in a growing number of occupations, you are nobody this side of a Ph.D. So how do you feel if you just don't happen to be college material, let alone Ph.D. material?

We claim, self-righteously, that ours is a classless society just because we have no hereditary aristocracy and no self-conscious proletariat. We pretend that America is all middle class. Even when some of our children drop out, because they wish to reject our middle class values, they do not start calling themselves lower class. Nor do the members of our power elite, the leaders of our military-industrial-governmental complex, call themselves upper class. They just are, except they do not use the word. So how do you feel, I ask again, if you know that you are outclassed?

And, of course, there is money, the ultimate criterion of success in our society. If competition is a little tin god for us, money — the reward of competition or, just as often, the reward for the successful elimination of competition — is our Golden Calf. The question "What is he worth?" does not apply to a man's human worth. It applies to his money worth. To be poor is not easy anywhere. In our country, however, it is uniquely humiliating. Among us, a poor person is always guilty until proved innocent. The burden of proof rests squarely and heavily upon the victim. How then are you likely to feel if you are barely making a living, let alone if you happen to be, heaven help you, on welfare? And perhaps homeless, or about to be made homeless, in midwinter?

### God's Verdict On The One-Talent Person
The one-talent man in the story symbolically represents the majority of Americans who are not Ph.D's, nor socially prominent, nor well-heeled.

The Master, in Jesus' parable, understood very well how the one-talent man felt and why he felt that way, but he did not show much patience with the fearfulness, the self-pity, the petulance, of the one-talent man.

"You knew!" the Master fairly hissed at the one-talent man. "You knew that I was not expecting miracles from you, only that you would take some normal risks and do an honest piece of work with what I had entrusted to you. You knew!"

As greeting-card trite as it may sound, there is something everyone can do. The person who is not Presidential timber can at least be an informed voter. The woman who cannot look like a siren does not have to look like a sloven. If you cannot compose music or even play an instrument, you can at least teach yourself to enjoy good music; and where would all the great composers and performers be if it were not for eager listeners?

Even people whose physical resources are severely limited — elderly people, handicapped people, sick people — can do a world of genuine good with what they have. There are important ministries open to persons with just one talent — or one-tenth of a talent. There is a political ministry of both criticism and commendation which requires only a telephone, or pen and paper, and a few stamps. There is a ministry of humor, which can help resolve anxious and often explosive situations with a joke and a laugh. And there is, of course, a ministry of prayer, which can accompany and undergird whatever else we do, and which remains available to us when we can do nothing else.

### Christian Faith And The One-Talent Person

Christian faith can work wonders for one-talent men and women. For example, Christian faith can help us be realistic about ourselves. We are not created equal. We are created with equal rights, and God loves each of us as if there were only one of us (Augustine). But we do not possess equal gifts. We are different: gloriously, disconcertingly different. This means, practically speaking, that some of us start out with a big bankroll while others come into the world under-capitalized. The less we pretend or mope about these facts of life, the less we will hurt.

Christian faith can also persuade us that, as Christians, we are not expected to be successful, only faithful. The two-talent man and the five-talent man received the same welcome from the Master. They had done what they could with what they had. The Master would have been equally pleased with the one-talent man, if only he had put this talent to work instead of burying it in a hole and crawling in after it!

But more is implied in the story. So far we have been talking about talents in terms of what we are born to or born with, most of which is not subject to change. But there is a great deal that is subject to change.

In the '50s, there was a Black woman in Montgomery, Alabama, by the name of Rosa Parks. She was a one-talent woman and, to the best of my knowledge, she was a model one-talent person, hard-working, thrifty, law-abiding. But deep inside her Rosa Parks had a quarrel: not with God, because of where God had put her, but with the White Man, because he was keeping her there, in her so-called place, sitting or standing up in the crowded back of the bus, while there were a dozen empty seats in the front. So Rosa

85

Parks, a one-talent child of God, sat down in one of those empty seats — and the rest is history.

Yes, Karl Marx was right: religion, indeed the Christian religion, has all too often served as the "opiate of the people." But the gospel is dynamite! The fuse may be long, but the explosive power is there and, in time, it will help tear down every system, every structure by means of which the Rosa Parkses of the world, God's own one-talent people, are being kept in their so-called place.

For Christian faith can give the one-talent person the critical insight and the moral strength to defy and overthrow oppression; and those of us who possess status, wealth, power — those of us with two talents or five talents — are not likely to be doing God's will if we merely double our own grubstake at the expense of the world's one-talent men and women. But that may be another parable.

Meanwhile, "to everyone who has, more will be given ... but from everyone who has not, even what he has will be taken away." That is the world's way. It certainly is the American way. But Christ's way is to expect more from those who have more and, in particular, to expect — and demand — justice, compassion, and an equal chance for those who have less.

For, under the gospel, having less does not mean being less. Amen.

# 8. Abraham And Sarah[1]

## *Introductory Note*

Abraham, the first Patriach, the "father of his people," is one of the most important figures in the Hebrew Bible as well as in the Christian Bible. What we read about him is likely to be part history, part legend, and we may never know the exact ratio between the two, nor does it ultimately matter: this is sacred history, the Word of God comes to us through the spoken and written words of men.

We have enough on record for a cycle of sermons about Abraham and his faithful Sarah. This is but a sample, based on a single, pivotal incident. The sermon starts with Abraham's laughter, and Sarah's, at the incredible announcement that they would at last have a child of their own, that long-desired son, at their respective ages of 100 and 90. The place of laughter in the Bible is briefly explored. So is laughing at "a word from the Lord," a high-risk act, it would seem. The final part homes in on the central message of the story: that, with God, it need never be too late — for anything.

This sermon also opens a rich vein for preaching on biblical personalities by exploring two or more of them at a time, in interaction. Here is a married couple: Abraham and Sarah. But there are also Esau and Jacob, brothers; Ruth and Naomi, daughter-in-law and mother-in-law; Peter, James, and John, the privileged Three among the Twelve; David and Absalom, father and son; the first group of deacons; and so on. In each case, focusing imaginatively on the humanity of the biblical characters will do much to arouse and sustain interest.

---

## *Scripture: Genesis 18:1-15*

Abraham and Sarah had been wanting a baby for ages. Not just any baby, either, but a baby boy, since girls did not count for much in those male chauvinist days. God kept appearing to Abraham and telling him that he would make Abraham the father of a great nation. But how could that be without at least one son?

When Sarah passed her womanly prime, she talked Abraham into having a son with Hagar, her maidservant; and when little Ishmael was born, Abraham and Sarah both forgot about having any children of their own. Sarah was simply too old and, after a few more decades, so was Abraham.

Then, when Abraham is ninety years old and Sarah well into her eighties, God appears once more and solemnly renews his promise. Abraham bursts out laughing! And, according to the parallel account in Genesis 18, Sarah, eavesdropping in the family tent, doubles up with silent, self-conscious laughter. Surely, God must be kidding!

### Laughter In The Bible

Laughter seems to be in short supply in the scriptures. In the Old Testament, we see God laughing at some of us but not with us. In Psalm 2, when the kings and rulers of the earth flex their muscles, threatening to topple God from his throne, the Psalmist assures us that "he who sits in the heavens laughs; the Lord holds them in derision."

The author of Psalm 59 has God laughing at his enemies who, he is certain, are also God's enemies. But that kind of laughter, whether God's or ours, is mirthless.

Ecclesiastes, in his great poem about time, allows that there is "a time to laugh" as well as "a time to weep," but his basic perception of life as "vanity" makes him much more at home with tears than with laughter. In fact, he declares that "sorrow is better than laughter, for by sadness of countenance the heart is made glad" (7:3)!

Only Second Isaiah, the nameless great prophet of the people's captivity in Babylon, strikes a clear and high note of joy. But that joy is all in the future. The present is grim. In fact, Second Isaiah's outbursts of joy are designed specifically to comfort his people in the midst of their grim life as strangers in a strange land.

But if there is little actual laughter in the Old Testament, there is a great deal of humor, both intentional and unintentional. Remember the scene in which Adam, having done wrong, hides from God — and God calls out, "Adam, where are you?" As if God did not know!

Remember Noah building the Ark in his backyard, miles away from the nearest body of water, ridiculously defensive with his curious, scoffing neighbors and foot-dragging wife and sons? And there is a great deal of humor in the story of the old couple, Abraham and Sarah, whom God is trying to persuade that, yes, they will have a son of their own, well after the biblical "threescore years and ten"; in fact, God insists that the little boy be named Isaac, which means "he laughs"!

A son of his people, nurtured on their ancient stories, Jesus himself reveals both a fine, quiet sense of humor and a healthy, masculine affirmation of life's common joys. His sense of humor surfaces again and again in his verbal duels with the Pharisees. One of his finest moments, for example, occurs when these solemn guardians of the Law are about to stone the woman taken in adultery — a thoroughly legal lynching. Jesus, being asked in mock deference what they ought to do with her (as if they did not know), doodles in the sand. Annoyed but curious, they peer over his shoulders. What is he writing? We don't know, but most likely he is writing: LOAN SHARK, and the crowd dwindles by three; BULLY, and five more men slink away; LECHER, and all the rest vanish, until there is only Jesus and the frightened woman. The rest of the story we know. The humor we may have overlooked.

But Jesus was surely a man of laughter as well as a keen and, at times, biting wit. He loved to party, usually with the wrong crowd, which was one of the reasons why the "right" people resented him so bitterly. At these parties — at the home of Zaccheus or Simon the Leper or in the Bethany household of Martha, Mary, and Lazarus — there was food and wine and laughter; and Jesus swapped stories and laughed with the rest. The Pharisees were killjoys; Jesus was a joy to have around. He was a one-man Psalm in praise of life, an incarnate *La Chaim*, the beautiful Jewish toast, "To life!"

Can you imagine Jesus sitting glumly, or even soberly, through the wedding at Cana? As if he had changed the water into vinegar instead of wine? No, the laughter of Jesus rings through all his days — until the very last week of his life. That is why the children loved him so: because he played with them, teased them, laughed with them. And when the disciples tried to keep the children away from him, Jesus said, "No! These children are closer to the Kingdom of God than any of you."

## Laughing At God?

So laughter is good, one of God's greatest gifts to us. But laughing at God? Surely that is something else!

Significantly, though, when Abraham and Sarah laugh at God's words, God does not strike them dead. On the contrary, in Genesis 17 God does not even seem to notice Abraham's laughing disbelief. God simply goes on to repeat his promise of a son. In Genesis 18, the divine messengers ("angels") do reprimand sputtering Sarah but oh! so gently. God clearly realizes that his promise must seem absurd! Who ever heard of an old woman having a baby? Anyone laughing at that notion surely would not mean any offense!

Abraham even tries to correct God — to correct his understanding of what he thought God was telling him, which did not make sense. "Oh, that Ishmael might live in thy sight!" Abraham cries out, still choking with laughter at the picture of his becoming a father, by Sarah, with 170 years between the two of them. But God is not referring to Ishmael. God is referring to a natural son yet unborn but to be born!

Going beyond the miracle, however, Abraham's laughter, and Sarah's, is actually a major compliment to God! What matters is not that Abraham and Sarah proved mistaken in their laughter but that they felt free to laugh! They knew that God was big enough and secure enough in his greatness that God would not be affronted, nor react with petty vindictiveness. Truly big people can always take a joke on themselves. Only small people, self-doubting, self-important people react peevishly when anyone is teasing them.

The laughter of Abraham and Sarah also reminds us that anyone who knows God, anyone who really walks with God, is entitled to a degree of loving familiarity with God. How trustingly Abraham bargains with God, when he is trying to save his nephew, Lot, from the impending destruction of Sodom! How does he dare? He does — because he knows God not only as all-mighty Creator and Ruler but also as a close personal Friend. This is what gave Abraham and Sarah the un-selfconscious *chutzpah* to laugh at God's promise of a son at their unlikely ages. They had walked with God all those eighty or ninety years. They knew God. They loved him, and they knew that he loved them.

## Is It Too Late?

If we take the story of the old couple literally, we are dealing with a miracle, a physical miracle. It is one of many in the Bible, and by no means the most remarkable one. But what sets this miracle apart is that it occurs in spite of Abraham's and Sarah's obvious and understandable unbelief!

Ordinarily, miracles demand belief — un-bending, soul-stirring belief — on the part of their beneficiaries. A miracle is supposed to be "an act of God triggered by the faith of a man or woman." So it is, in nearly all cases in Scriptures. But in this case God's purpose overrules even his usual demand for belief. God's faith in Abraham, and in the rightness of his selection of Abraham as the father of his people, allows God to overlook Abraham's temporary lapse of faith in him. God has resolved that it is not too late for Abraham and Sarah to fulfill their destiny by having a son of their own. It does not matter that Abraham and Sarah believe, plausibly, that it is too late.

Can we ever be sure that it really is too late? Most of us who profess faith in God and in his power do not really apply that faith to ourselves, especially when it comes to life's most common fact, aging. In our youth-ridden culture, aging is treated as a thing to hide; and being old can be a source of severe guilt, as if it were a crime.

But we who are getting older or are perhaps old, at whatever age, have largely ourselves to blame. Too long have we subscribed to bruising cliches like the one about age forty which a friend sent me on a birthday card when I turned forty: "Remember, after forty we do fewer and fewer things for the first time and more and more things for the last time!" With a friend like that, who needs enemies?

So I say, "Rubbish!" Thomas Hardy felt burned out as a novelist in his fifties. That was all he knew how to do: write novels. But what did he do? He began writing poetry! And in what turned out to be the final third of his life, he became a major poet, with a reputation approximating his deservedly formidable reputation as a novelist. He simply refused to lie down and die when it seemed time to do so. He refused to believe that it was too late to start something new.

I don't know enough about Grandma Moses. I don't know what she did before her sixties or thereabouts or what she was like. But I do know, as we all do, that long past the age when it makes sense to begin painting, with arthritis no doubt gnawing at her joints, Grandma Moses took up painting and became a significant "primitive" painter. She did not know enough to lie down and die, either. She also refused to believe that it was too late — and proved that it was not!

By cooperating with God's life-affirming love, miracles of productivity and mature fulfillment are possible not just after forty, but even after eighty. "You are as young as you feel" is only half true, because you may be feeling rotten. But you are as young as your faith is strong — your faith in yourself. And your faith in yourself will be the strongest, most stable, most death-defying, if it is grounded in faith in God — and in the faith God has in you, if only you give God a chance!

Physical miracles, intellectual miracles, and, yes, moral and spiritual miracles are possible within God's power and love. When Nicodemus asked Jesus about the "second birth," "How can that be? Can a man return into his mother's womb and start all over?" he was not being impudent. No, Nicodemus was being profoundly wistful. His problem was not that he had been a flop until then. By all worldly reckoning, Nicodemus had been a success: a man of wealth and status, a member of the Sanhedrin, even a good man. But Nicodemus was not satisfied. He longed for that mysterious "second birth" Jesus was talking about. But he thought that it was too late!

Jesus disagreed. "The spirit of God works where God chooses," he said. God can work miracles of renewal in us if we are really in earnest about seeking such a miracle. It does not matter how many years have passed or what painful losses we have sustained. The Spirit of God can blow new life into dead bones, if God decides that they shall live — if they themselves truly want to live again.

Abraham and Sarah, though very close to God, were not very wise at the moment of our story. They did not believe that God really meant what he was telling them: how could he? But they were proved wrong — by God's overriding grace.

We, knowing the story, can be wiser. We can thank God that, with him, it need never be too late, that, with God, a new beginning is always possible.

---

1. Previously published in *Adam and Eve and You* (Omega Press, 1977). Copyright John R. Bodo.

# 9. Demetrius' Brother

## Introductory Note

This sermon deals with a biblical character who is not in the Bible. Not by name. Not even by direct inference. So the question is: can we justify inventing a brother for Demetrius and inserting him into the story of the riot at Ephesus told in Acts, chapter 19?

Paul and his coworkers get in trouble in Ephesus for denouncing the worship of the goddess Diana as idolatry. Demetrius, leader of the union of silversmiths, whose livelihood depends on Diana, whips up the crowd. Paul and company escape; they can move on and they do. But how would a silversmith of Ephesus fare if he had become a Christian during Paul's brief stay?

Philotheos ("Phil" for us), Demetrius' twin, a silversmith converted by Paul, must now decide whether he can go on making a living on the cult of an idol or whether his commitment to Jesus Christ demands that he quit. And if he must quit, what next? What about his wife, his children, his mortgage?

Shuttling between the historic and the deliberately anachronistic, we follow Phil to a moral victory, only to be reminded that God offers no safe conduct to the faithful. Anyone who tries to apply his Christian faith to his daily work risks being eaten alive just like the early Christians, though in the office or the factory rather than the arena.

---

## Scripture: Acts 19:23-41

The riot was over. The wise words of the Town Clerk had proved effective. The crowd dispersed. To the rank and file of the silversmiths and of all the other craftsmen and businessmen of Ephesus,

95

Jesus remained an obscure and vaguely threatening figure. They had been reassured but not enlightened. No one had risen to challenge their religious and economic system in his name.

Paul had been prevented from attending. His two helpers, Gaius and Aristarchus, had not been given a chance to state their case. And now everybody was going home, perhaps a trifle uneasy but ready to forget the whole thing. The next item on the agenda was business as usual.

But there was one man in that crowd who could not forget. His name did not get into the Bible, but he was there. I know that he was there. So we shall give him a name. We shall call him Philotheos, "Lover of God." But that is too much of a mouthful, so we'll call him Phil for short: Phil of Ephesus. And at no extra charge, we'll make him the twin brother of Demetrius. Why not? We may even find out that he is our twin brother, too.

Phil was also a silversmith in Ephesus. He was a fine craftsman and an astute businessman. He had been successful enough so that now he was able to work personally only on the most challenging orders while letting his contractors and subcontractors attend to the routine work. He was a member in good standing of the guild, dependable, respected by his fellows.

Phil had heard the harangue of his brother, Demetrius, but he had not joined in the shouting because, earlier that week, something had happened to him. He had chanced into a meeting of the followers of Jesus and listened to his story as presented by a Jew called Paul. Phil had heard the gospel, the Good News of God's Kingdom, and his heart had responded. He had accepted this Jesus as his Master and Lord. But now he wondered. He wondered what this decision would cost him as a silversmith.

Phil was a realist. He did not fail to grasp the obvious truth of Demetrius' opening gambit: "Men, you know that from this business we have our wealth." The great temple of Diana at Ephesus was one of the Seven Wonders of the World. According to tradition, gold instead of mortar had been used to join together the marble blocks of the giant octagonal structure which covered an acre and a half of ground. Silver, the most precious metal next to gold, had been just as lavishly used. The silversmiths of Ephesus had done well at the construction of the temple and had been doing well ever since. Thanks to the tourist trade, the demand for little silver likenesses of the temple and of the goddess was insatiable. Anything that threatened the cult of Diana, threatened the livelihood of hundreds of silversmiths as well as thousands of other workers in related trades and crafts. To this extent, Demetrius was right.

But, Phil mused on, Demetrius had not been content to point out the obvious economic implications of the gospel for Ephesus. He had touched his fellow guild members quickly on this most sensitive point but had moved on, at once, to loftier considerations. "There is danger," Demetrius said, "not only that this trade of ours may come into disrepute, but also that the temple of the great goddess Diana may count for nothing, and that she may even be deposed from her magnificence — she whom all Asia and the whole world worship!"

Phil was no historian but he had intuition. He sensed that this was probably not the first time in history, nor the last, that patriotism and religion were being invoked on behalf of economic vested interests. Phil half admired Demetrius for his subtle switch from the real, down-to-earth reason for his opposition to the gospel to this noble, flag-waving defense of the great goddess Diana, private deity of the Ephesians, to whom worshipers from all over the world paid homage — directly into the pockets of the tradesmen and businessmen of Ephesus!

Phil did not know, could not know, at the time his heart responded to the claim of Jesus of Nazareth, that he was going to run such awesome risks. Religious non-conformity was one thing. Being accused of un-Ephesian activities was something else. But being classified as a person suspect both religiously and politically was almost too much to face!

For Demetrius and the guild of silversmiths had considerable power over their members. If Phil incurred their wrath, he might be warned at first, then boycotted, so that his profits would fall off, then squeezed out of business altogether. There might also be "accidents" to himself and his employees, and social ostracism as painful as physical violence. Clearly, if Phil knew what was good for him and for his business, he would not worry too much about relating his faith in Jesus Christ to the practice of his trade. He would stifle his misgivings and perhaps give ten percent of his earnings to the little community of Christians.

Now if Phil had been a bachelor, his dilemma might not have been so acute. At least he would have had only himself to consider. A man is more likely to make costly decisions on moral grounds if he is risking only his own neck. But Phil was a family man. He had a wife and two point two children who depended on him. Furthermore, the family had recently moved from downtown Ephesus to one of the better suburbs, because Phil felt that his wife and children deserved a healthier environment than the little apartment behind the expanding workshop. What with mortgage payments and the expense of additional and more elegant furniture, Phil could ill afford to take the kind of risk which standing up for his new faith might entail. His responsibility to his wife and children suggested extreme caution.

Then, too, Phil was a responsible employer. He estimated that, if he were forced out of business for taking a Christian stand on this matter of idolatry and profit, his employees would lose their jobs, too. Granted that they were competent workers who could probably get other jobs, the question remained whether, having been associated with a religiously and politically tainted character, they might not have a very hard time finding work. Phil did not know the Greek phrase for "guilt by association," but he was quite aware of the reality. He guessed that his younger and more highly skilled employees would probably be forgiven and hired, but he was doubtful about the chances of his older, semi-skilled and un-skilled workers for whom changing jobs might be difficult, even without any added complications.

Phil was deadlocked. He could go neither forward nor backward. It seemed impossible for him to pretend that nothing had happened to him earlier that week — that the story of Jesus of Nazareth was just a beautiful, wishful tale or that the Lord, while perhaps risen, and alive, was not really concerned with how Phil was making a living. No, Phil knew even at this kindergarten stage of his faith, that Jesus cannot be kept out of any part of a man's life — that nothing is insignificant or morally neutral in his sight —

that all economic, social, political actions are subject to the close and revealing scrutiny of the Master. So Phil realized that the most tempting option — going back to business as usual — was really no option at all. Having once glimpsed the truth, God's own down-to-earth Truth, in Jesus, Phil knew that he could never again live within the accepted web of lies.

The only other option seemed to be to quit. Phil thought that perhaps he could ease out of the production of silver temples and goddesses and develop instead a new line of silver tableware or other non-controversial products. Or else he might try to make a slow if painful switch to some other entirely different occupation. But even this option proved unacceptable to Phil's new standards as a disciple of Jesus of Nazareth.

Phil realized that removing himself from an immoral system would do him little good in the eyes of God if he left the system itself unchallenged. It was the system that had to go — the popular idolatry with all its phony patriotic and religious sanctions and slogans. And there was no one outside the system who could more effectively challenge it in the name of Jesus Christ than an insider. In other words, Phil.

This discovery marked a new beginning for Phil. As soon as he found out that he had to follow his new Master not by leaving behind the dangerous implications of his faith for his daily work but by going right back to his workshop, his guild, his service club, Phil felt relieved, immensely relieved. At least he was not going to run away! With his new Master's help, he was going to try to introduce into the immoral economics of the system the moral power of the Master's life and death! For the first time in his life, Phil felt that he was in the world for a reason, for a purpose other than just surviving. For the first time, he knew a sense of calling, of real vocation, and not just as a Christian-in-general but pointedly, specifically, as a Christian craftsman, a Christian businessman, a Christian silversmith!

A second discovery followed at once. At the meeting of the Christians on the riverbank at the outskirts of town, Phil had noticed a couple of familiar faces. He had not been the only silversmith there. There had been at least two others, lesser men in the

99

guild who right now were probably going through the same pangs of conscience, and who would probably look to him for leadership if only he would show his colors to them and take them into his confidence.

What was it the Master had said? "Where two or three are gathered in my name, there am I in the midst of them." Well, perhaps by seeking out those two fellow silversmiths and sharing his fears and hopes with them, they might be led to discover others. Maybe there were scores of craftsmen and businessmen caught in the system of profitable idol-making, longing for release, ready to face the cost in the name of the Master who would claim their whole life — religious, economic, political — until the whole city of Ephesus felt the impact, the extraordinary impact, which a handful of transformed persons can make upon any sluggish, stagnant majority.

And here began Phil's third and greatest discovery. Suddenly he realized that all his life he had been a prisoner of fear: not of any concrete fear but of a vague, diffuse fear — fear of what people might say or think if he permitted himself just one unorthodox, unconventional move! For the sake of his business, for the sake of his good standing in his guild and club, Phil had allowed himself to become less than himself: a look-alike man leading a look-alike life! Always he had been with the majority, a chip off the huge, dull block of Ephesian respectability: prosperous and worried, gregarious and lonely, successful and futile. But now Phil saw a new horizon. It was a horizon overhung with dark, heavy clouds, but a horizon illumined even then by the brightness of the Master's promise of help and power!

Phil of Ephesus had no clear-cut plan. He was just at the beginning of his pilgrimage, but he was equipped with the essentials: a heart committed to Jesus Christ; a conviction that the Master wanted him to make his witness as a silversmith in the face of the assembled forces of Ephesian money-patriotism and money-religion; and a brave hope that this meager strength, reinforced by the strength of a tiny but growing number of sympathizers among his fellow-silversmiths, would be sufficient for the task. For the first time in his life, Phil was not paralyzed by statistics, forecasts, polls, and graphs. Now he knew that, when justice and truth are at stake, one person — or two or three — *and Jesus Christ* are more than a majority.

Brave words, aren't they?

But I wish I knew the end of the story.

I wish I could assure you that Phil won his fight without harm to himself or his loved ones; that his business, after a few jolts, was reorganized and flourished more than ever; and that the whole city of Ephesus, purged of the goddess of Diana and all her hangers-on, lived happily ever after!

But the plain truth is: *I do not know.*

Diana, and the system which fed upon her cult, vanished, to be sure. But so did Phil. How big a part Phil played in the downfall of the system, I do not know. Perhaps Phil barely made a dent in the system, before it caught up with him and crucified him.

But so what?

If a cross was good enough for Jesus of Nazareth, should it not be good enough for Phil of Ephesus? Or Phil of (*name of your city*)?

# 10. Judas The Villain[1]

## *Introductory Note*

Judas probably qualifies as the most hated and despised man in history, at least in Christian history. His betrayal of our Lord has been dealt with in countless sermons and works of art. Few have even tried to find the man, the human being, behind the despicable deed, while admitting to a measure of perplexity as to the motive or motives behind the deed.

This sermon is somewhat different in that an attempt is made to see Judas, the traitor, through the eyes of Jesus, the victim. While it seems presumptuous to assume that we might figure out how our Lord felt about Judas, we have tried to keep our hypothesis, that Jesus loved Judas and forgave him, solidly grounded in the Gospel narratives.

The substitution of "son of waste" for "son of perdition" (John 17:12) might not by itself justify our hypothesis. It does, however, strengthen and lend poignancy to the argument, especially when we recall Luther's translation of the expression as "lost child." We are not trying to whitewash Judas or minimize the enormity of his action. Rather we are exalting the spirit of our Lord who, in the midst of his dying agony, prayed for forgiveness for all his enemies. Including Judas, the villain.

---

## *Scripture: Matthew 26:14-25; 27:1-5*

In Dante's *Inferno*, the lowest pit of hell is not the hottest but the coldest place. It is a frozen lake composed of human tears. In this lake lives Satan, a hideous monster with three heads. In each mouth, he is crushing a traitor: Brutus and Cassius on the right and

103

on the left and, in the central mouth, Judas Iscariot. No other literary or artistic image expresses more strikingly the horror in which Judas has been held through the ages. No parents would name a son Judas. No one would inflict the name even on a stray dog.

But this Judas, this embodiment of treachery, was also a man — flesh of our flesh, bone of our bone. What is more remarkable, he was one of the men whom Jesus had called to special privilege. Three times in the Passion narrative, Matthew refers to Judas as "one of the Twelve," as if he could hardly believe it himself. Whatever Judas became, a mere three years earlier he had been a person of sufficient promise both to receive and to accept the call of Jesus Christ.

## Judas The Man

What do we know about this man Judas? The Evangelists do not tell us very much apart from his performance as a traitor. They can hardly be blamed for their silence. They could not and would not look beyond the vileness of his treason. Wherever Judas is mentioned, it is in the context of disapproval and contempt. In fact, he is never mentioned at all without some reference to his treason. He is "Judas Iscariot ... (who also betrayed him)." He is "Judas who betrayed him." It is nearly impossible to catch a reliable view of a person through such a dark curtain of hate.

If you want to track down all the references in all four Gospels to the background and character of Judas, you would be even more perplexed because of the man's extraordinary ordinariness. He was a Judean surrounded by eleven Galileans. As a one-man minority, he might well be carrying a chip on his shoulder. It seems, too, that he was rather smart and therefore jealous of the others, especially of Peter, James, and John, who occupied favored places within the circle of the disciples.

There appears to be a dependable consensus that Judas was good with money, or loved money, or most likely both. Still, thirty silver coins in the currency of the day would be too paltry a sum to motivate him or anyone to commit such a gross act of treason just for the money.

But if money was not the motive, what was? Scholars have been trying to unravel the motivation of Judas, the traitor, but have not come up with anything conclusive. The most widely accepted hypothesis seems to be that Judas was a Zealot, a member of that small, violent sect of super-patriots who wanted to free their people from the yoke of Rome by revolution. Judas had his heart set on Jesus' leading that revolution. He wanted Jesus to become "King of the Jews." When at last he understood that Jesus did not seek that kind of kingdom, and that violence was abhorrent to him, Judas betrayed him. Whether out of pain or out of spite or in order to force Jesus to embrace the revolution after all if only to save his own life, Judas acted. We can only conjecture why. We simply do not know which of these motives or what combination of them moved him to do what he did.

What exactly did Judas do? He promised the Jewish religious authorities, the High Priest and his forces, to deliver Jesus to them. The High Priest wanted Jesus out of the way, because Jesus was gaining a large following which the Romans might interpret as the beginning of another Jewish revolt.

The Romans knew how to deal with Jewish revolts. They had put down a number of them recently by proceeding with the utmost ruthlessness not just against the revolutionaries but against the entire Jewish people. Caiaphas wanted to protect his people against another abortive revolt and the ghastly reprisals that would follow, but he dared not try to arrest Jesus in broad daylight, when the Master was surrounded by large, friendly crowds. Judas' offer was most welcome, for Judas promised the High Priest's cohorts to let them know where Jesus would be the next time he withdrew from the crowds. And that is what Judas did, quite promptly.

## Jesus And Judas

Judas was a rather ordinary traitor, then. Only his victim was extraordinary. In fact, I don't think that we can see either the traitor or the act of treason clearly, until we look at them through the eyes of the betrayed.

How did Jesus feel about Judas? According to one version, advocated by the author of the Fourth Gospel, Jesus picked Judas in the first place because the plot called for a villain. It is true that the manner in which the plot unfolds in the Gospels, especially in the Fourth Gospel, makes Jesus' betrayal by Judas an essential part of the plot. But to credit Jesus with such advance knowledge undermines his real humanity — without which both the cross and the empty tomb lose their meaning. When the Evangelist John suggests that Jesus chose Judas, because someone had to play the traitor's part, he means to exalt Jesus. But he misses the mark, because anything that makes Jesus less than fully human, debases him.

No, Jesus picked Judas because Judas showed promise as well as zeal. Then, when the pressure rose, one man out of twelve was bound to break — if only by the law of human averages. In a sense, they all betrayed the Master. Peter, the only one who drew a sword in his defense, soon denied ever having known him. The ten others faded into the night. Eventually, John alone was present in Caiaphas' court.

Until the very end, then, Judas had indeed been "one of the Twelve," no less human than the rest of them. And Jesus probably loved Judas, as offensive as this might sound, just as he loved the others, in the intimacies of their spiritual apprenticeship, in the excitement of their early apostolic ventures, and in the tension of the steady march of events.

Then, at the Last Supper, Jesus knew. How he had discovered the dreadful truth about Judas we do not know, but it could not have been very difficult. It was probably all over Judas' face, except for the specific details of time and place. So, as much to console the eleven as to give the traitor a twinge of sorrow, Jesus said, "The Son of Man goes as it is written of him, but woe to that man by whom the Son of Man is betrayed! It would have been better for that man if he had not been born!" (Matthew 26:24).

There is something movingly deliberate and willing about the Master's surrender to his destiny. Neither Judas nor anyone else can take from him that which he will freely give. The Son of Man sees the shadow of death and advances unafraid; but woe to him who will soon wish that he had never been born, who will do his gruesome best to make believe he never was born!

There is no trace of bitterness in Jesus, only the bitter taste of the cup which, for the sake of his mission, he must drain to the dregs. When Judas approaches with the armed mob and kisses the Master in the ghostly light of the torches, Jesus asks, "Friend, why are you here?" (Matthew 26:50). "Friend!" Jesus is turning the knife in the wound, but his blade is clean. Even the pain he inflicts has a cleansing, surgical effect on the festering conscience of Judas. That word "friend" — and the smile that accompanies it — propels Judas into a frenzy of remorse and out into the dark night of death, so that the most damned death occurs at the same time as the most saving death!

## Perhaps A Clue

But there is still a word to be spoken, a word from the cross. Did Jesus include Judas in his last prayer, "Father, forgive them, for they know not what they do?" In a sense, Judas did not deserve to be included since, of all people, he knew what he had done. But does anyone deserve to be included in that prayer? Does anyone deserve to be forgiven by the Crucified?

We do not know, we cannot know, whether Jesus meant to include Judas, specifically, in his prayer on the cross. But there is one fleeting clue, in the Gospel of John of all places, that suggest that Jesus did mean to forgive Judas, and especially Judas. In what came to be known as his High-Priestly Prayer (John, chapter 17) Jesus prays, speaking of his disciples: " I have guarded them, and none of them is lost but the son of perdition" (John 17:12).

Thus the usual translation. But the basic meaning of the Greek word rendered as "perdition" is not "damnation" but "destruction" or "waste." Perhaps Jesus remembered how Judas had used this very word while ranting about the waste of the perfume that a woman, perhaps Mary Magdalene, had poured over the Master in an act of beautiful, foolish devotion. Could it be that the disciple most worried about waste had himself become the one waste product of the Master's love? "Son of perdition" does not sound like Jesus. "Son of waste" does. Indeed, Martin Luther follows the purest evangelical instinct when he translates the phrase as "lost child"!

What would be more like Jesus than a prayer for Judas: "Father, forgive thy lost child"?

Perhaps I have carried this plea for the ordinariness, the humanity, the forgivability of Judas too far. You may not be able to identify with Judas at all, and may therefore resent my apparent defense of him. But remember: if you cannot identify with Judas, you must be a better person than any one of the disciples!

How so?

Because, at the Last Supper, when Jesus quietly announced, "One of you is going to betray me," the disciples did not point at Judas. They did not even look in his direction. They looked at Jesus and, in the full terror of self-knowledge, they asked him, every one for himself: "Is it I, Lord?"

---

1. From *A Gallery of New Testament Rogues* by John R. Bodo. ©1979. The Westminster Press. Used by permission of Westminster John Knox Press.

# 11. Women In Paul's Life

## *Introductory Note*

This sermon is as much about Paul as it is about the women in his life: women whom he converted; women, some of whom became valued partners in his mission and ministry. The main object is to correct the impression, so widespread and so hard to dislodge, that Paul was a misogynist who grossly discriminated against women.

While acknowledging and reviewing Paul's most notorious anti-woman statements, we explore the character and values of Paul as a child of his time and culture, arguing that, by the standards of his time and culture, he was remarkably open to women, treating them as persons, entrusting important assignments to them.

A minor but important object of the sermon is to sketch the biblical basis for "Women's Lib." Of course, the biblical case for the full acceptance of women as men's equals needs to be made primarily from Jesus' teachings and his dealings with women. However, it is amazing how positive a case can be made from the writings of Paul, the "whipping boy of Women's Lib"!

---

## *Scripture: Romans 16:1-4; Acts 16:11-15; 18:1-4*

As a rule, every movement has at least one patron saint and one whipping boy. I do not know of any one person who qualifies as the patron saint of the Women's Liberation Movement. I do know that the title of "Whipping Boy of Women's Lib" belongs, uncontested, to the Apostle Paul.

Paul's image as a hater and oppressor of women is not an invention of Women's Lib. Thoughtful women, Christian women,

109

cling to this impression of the Apostle. And Christian men, anxious to help secure for women, for the first time in history, the status of complete human beings, tend to accept the image uncritically.

The surface evidence against Paul is so convincing to twentieth-century readers that we seldom bother to look beneath the surface: to review Paul's dealings with and attitude toward women in the context of the first century in which Paul lived.

## The Evidence Against Paul

One way to make a women-hater of Paul is to assert that he never married, or that he was impotent, or both. There is no basis whatsoever for either assertion.

We have no reference to Paul's being or having been married. However, that does not mean that he was not married! If Peter's mother-in-law had not been taken ill and then healed by Jesus, we would have not known that Peter was married either! The Christian Church emerged in a heavily patriarchal society, whether Jewish or Greco-Roman. When the life of a man was being chronicled, his wife might not even be mentioned! But that did not mean that he did not have a wife or that he and his wife did not have a tender, beautiful union.

In Paul's case, it is indeed more likely that he was not married. Paul was a Pharisee; and, while the Pharisees were not committed to celibacy, they were in a sense secular monks. If you decided to devote your life to the perfect fulfillment of God's Law, you might not have time for marriage.

But that would not in any way suggest that there was anything wrong with Paul as a man. Our contemporary obsession notwithstanding, it is possible for a man to live without sex without being either abnormal or sexless. And the notion that Paul's "thorn in the flesh" was a euphemism for chronic impotence is just too far-fetched to merit attention!

But the chief reason why Paul has been credited, or debited, with being a hater and oppressor of women can be found in his writings, specifically in three passages.

The first passage is 1 Corinthians 11:2-16, where Paul lays down, or rather confirms, the rule that women must not uncover their heads in church. He goes on to defend this rule with some very quaint, antique exegesis of Old Testament texts. The point is plain and, understandably, leaves us cold.

The second passage is 1 Timothy 2:8-15. Here again Paul stresses the need for modesty in women's dress and conduct, but he also goes further. "I permit no women to teach or to have authority over men," he writes to his disciple, Timothy. There is no denying that Paul accepted the traditional Hebrew "hierarchy of beings" with God at the top, followed by the angels, followed by Man, that is, the male of the species, with Woman at the lowest rank.

The third passage is 1 Corinthians 14:34-35, where Paul says flatly that women should not even speak in church but should discuss their questions with their husbands, at home, "for it is shameful for a woman to speak in church."

It is silly even to try to deny the patriarchal bias of Paul. He was a child of his time and place, just as we are children of our time and place. Jesus himself, in his humanity, was a child of his time and place. He believed that the earth was flat. What else could he believe?

For example, if Paul argued that women should keep their heads covered in the worship assemblies of Christians, we might note that it was rather liberal that they were there in the first place. In the Ancient World, religion was largely for men. Women were excluded from the gatherings of most of the religious communities which flourished in the Roman Empire in Paul's day. By contrast, the Early Church carried on the far more liberal practice of the Jews by including women.

Again, if Paul argued that women should not teach, that is, "prophesy," in the worship assemblies, the very argument proves not only that they were at least there but that they felt free to speak up, which was unheard of, even among Jews! In other words, the gospel which Paul was preaching, the gospel which gave rise to little churches throughout the then-known world, had already begun

111

to act as a liberating ferment! Can we blame Paul for being somewhat anxious to control the process of fermentation?

And this leads us to Paul's strongest statement about women: that they should keep silent in the worship assemblies, that is, refrain not only from teaching but from saying anything at all. Well and good. But let us remind ourselves of the real subject of 1 Corinthians 14 and, for that matter, of the two other offending passages. The real subject of these passages was not women: it was chaos and, in particular, sexual license carried on under the banner of religion.

This was what Paul had to contend with in the little churches he had founded, especially in Corinth — the Tenderloin, the Barbary Coast, of Greece! Surrounded by cults which were designed chiefly to dignify, to "baptize," the grossest sexual promiscuity, Paul could hardly be expected to cheer when women first began to speak up, and then to whoop it up, in the Corinthian congregation and elsewhere. Observing what went on in some of the temples of the Gentiles, Paul was afraid that some of the converts from these cults would drag the infant church down the pagan road to hell. And they nearly did.

## Paul's Gracious Words

Yes, Paul was a child of his time and place, Jewish and patriarchal. Yes, Paul was afraid that the "emancipation" of women in the churches might result in the perversion of Christian liberty into license. And, yes, Paul knew what he was talking about, because he had not walked the streets of Corinth, or of any other pagan city, with his eyes closed.

But, along with his severe words about what he regarded as unseemly conduct for Christian women, Paul also had some beautiful, gracious words for women, especially for Christian women.

In Colossians 3:18-21, Paul admonishes wives to be "subject to your husbands as is fitting in the Lord"; but he adds at once, "Husbands, love your wives and do not be harsh with them!" That was *news*! The very suggestion of mutuality of obligation, whether for husbands and wives, or for parents and children or, even more startling, for masters and slaves, was news — brave, liberating news!

And, should you accept the General Letter to the Ephesians as a letter of Paul, you would find there, in Chapter 5, verses 21-33, the most beautiful picture of Christ's relationship with the church drawn in terms of the mutual love of husband and wife! No hater or oppressor of women could have written that passage, nor the passage from Colossians 3! I would go even further. I would say that such a glowing account of the love of husband and wife could be written only by one who had either been happily married himself or who had at least experienced, in his childhood, the shared love of his father and mother!

And to those passages we must add, of course, one of the greatest statements of Paul, Galatians 3:27-28, the Magna Carta of Christian liberty: "For as many of you as were baptized into Christ have put on Christ. There is neither Jew nor Greek, there is neither slave nor free, there is neither male nor female; for you are all one in Jesus Christ." Does this sound like the words of a man who hated and oppressed women?

### Paul's Gracious Acts

But to get to know the real Paul with respect to women, we have to talk about not just what he said but what he did. Specifically, we have to conjure up a few of the many women in Paul's life. Not in his "love life," of course, since we know nothing about that part of his life, but in his work life, which was really Paul's whole life after he became an apostle of Jesus Christ.

Of the two dozen women mentioned in connection with Paul in the Acts of the Apostles or by Paul himself in his Epistles, we shall recall only three: Lydia, Prisca (or Priscilla), and Phoebe. Each of these women is somehow symbolic of the unknown Paul, the Paul we have tended to ignore, the Paul who loved persons, many of whom were women.

Lydia was a native of Asia Minor (now Turkey), who moved to Philippi, a major city in Macedonia (now Northern Greece), where she prospered in the garment industry. While in Philippi, Lydia became a "worshiper of God" which, in the language of the

New Testament, means a Gentile attached to a synagogue to study Judaism, contemplating conversion to Judaism.

After hearing Paul preach, by the riverside on the outskirts of Philippi where the Jews had a place of prayer, Lydia became a convert to Christianity, Paul's first convert in Europe. No sooner converted, Lydia offered Paul and his associates her hospitality so that her home became the first Christian church in Europe. Do you think Lydia would have responded to Paul in this way if Paul had been "putting her down" because she was "just a woman"?

Prisca, or Priscilla, was a Roman lady of noble family married to a Jewish craftsman name Aquila. Expelled from Rome by the Emperor Claudius, one of Hitler's many spiritual ancestors, the Jews of Rome fled wherever they could. Prisca and her husband did not stop until they reached Corinth, where they met Paul. Converted by Paul, they invited him to stay with them, which made sense since Aquila's trade, like Paul's, was tentmaking, leather work; in fact, Aquila and Priscilla opened a leather shop in Corinth with Paul as a somewhat intermittent partner.

Before long, the couple took their place among Paul's most valued co-workers in evangelism. Following Paul to Ephesus, Priscilla and her husband nearly lost their lives in some danger they shared with Paul, probably the great riot of the silversmiths. And wherever they settled, their home served as a Christian church.

Priscilla's service to Paul and to the gospel would have justified singling her out for attention in any case. But the main reason for singling her out in this study of Paul and women is that, in the Acts of the Apostles, she is frequently mentioned ahead of her husband — "Prisca and Aquila" rather than "Aquila and Priscilla." This may be merely a recognition of her upper class background. Far more likely, however, it is an acknowledgement of her superior Christian service. Now I ask you: could any woman have so distinguished herself if Paul had simply sat on all women?

Finally, there is Phoebe, a resident of Cenchrae, Corinth's big seaport. A woman of wealth, Phoebe is on record as having helped countless persons in need even before she became a Christian. After her conversion, Phoebe earned the title of deaconess — and that was news! She was the first woman to receive the title hitherto reserved for men. And Paul speaks of Phoebe not only in terms of her high status in the church, but as "our sister," a term of affection he uses sparingly!

Most important, when Paul completed his Epistle to the Romans, his greatest work and one of the greatest theological treatises ever written, it was Phoebe who carried it to Rome for him. In a day when travel took a hundred times longer and was far more dangerous, would an unfeeling male chauvinist, a hater and oppressor of women, entrust the crowning work of his life — and, no doubt, the only copy, since this was before Xerox or IBM — to a mere woman?

Young Saul, growing up in Tarsus, in a devout Jewish home, learned early in life the traditional Jewish prayer: "I thank Thee, Lord, that Thou hast not made me a woman"! We should not hold it against Paul that he did not jump out of his century straight into ours! Rather, we should be grateful to Paul for so wondrously spreading the gospel's liberating contagion, which even now is working itself out, both within and beyond the churches, in the ongoing movement of human liberation, of which women's liberation is a large and integral part.

# 12. Amos

## Introductory Note

Amos is arguably the greatest prophet of social justice in the Bible and perhaps in all history. The clarity with which he perceives and sets forth God's priorities is unsurpassed. His denunciation of the wealthy and the powerful who oppress God's poor is violent. It is also sublime poetry from the lips of an unschooled, perhaps illiterate shepherd. His indictment of the religious establishment, personified by the high priest Amaziah, is devastating. We do not know how long he lived, nor how he died, but it would be straining our credulity to be told that he died a natural death!

The sermon is hardly a personality profile; we know too little about the man. However, to the extent that Amos was wholly identified with his prophetic mission, we probably know as much as we need to know, as much as he himself would care to have us know.

The offense of Amos is matched only by his relevance, which he shall retain as long as there are Christians (and Jews and Muslims) who distinguish, by whatever words, between a "personal" and a "social" gospel or moral standard. As long as this self-serving view persists anywhere, Amos will be there to challenge, expose, and destroy it in the name of God whose priorities continue to be justice and compassion.

---

## Scripture: The Book of Amos

In the middle of the eighth century, B.C., the Jewish nation was divided. There was a Southern Kingdom, Judah, with Jerusalem as its capital. And there was a Northern Kingdom, Israel, with the city of Samaria as its capital.

Amos hailed from the South. He was a shepherd or sheep rancher from Tekoa, a village in the desert south of Jerusalem. During one of his trips north, however, he exploded over what he observed in Israel's thriving cities: in Samaria, in Gilgal, in Bethel.

A clash with Amaziah, the High Priest of the Northern Kingdom, resulted in Amos' banishment from Israel. Most likely he was bodily deported to his native Judah, only a day's journey away. For all we know, he never returned to Israel. But his prophecies, uttered around 750 B.C., came true within a quarter century. Assyria overran Israel. In 722, the capital city, Samaria, was destroyed. From the occupied Northern Kingdom, thousands of Jews were carried away to Assyria, as captives.

### The Offense Of Amos

But why was there such a fuss over Amos and his preaching? *Amos gave offense by who he was.*

He was a shepherd, not a priest, not a scribe. And while all prophets were not necessarily priests or scribes, they were supposed to have acceptable credentials of one kind or another. Amos had none. Furthermore, he was a quasi-foreigner. While all Jews knew themselves to be Jews and recognized one another as Jews, the divided kingdom was in effect two nations, each with its own king. Amos was welcome in Israel as long as he minded his own business.

*Amos also gave offense by how he said what he said.* It takes a special gift to say nasty things nicely. Amos did not have that gift, nor did he care to cultivate it. He had nasty things to say, and he went out of his way to say them as nastily as possible. The fact that he was a great poet as well as a great prophet did not help matters. The people of Israel, who were enjoying a time of peace and unaccustomed prosperity, would not put up with such speech.

But it was *what Amos said* that gave the greatest offense. What he said went far beyond specific social criticism. In his preaching, Amos challenged his people's entire self-image, by challenging their image of God.

For example, the Jews believed that Jehovah was their God and only theirs. Were they not his Chosen People? Amos, however, dared to suggest that God's judgment upon nations is impartial; that the Jews, the kingdoms of Judah and of Israel, were as much subject to God's Judgment as were the heathen Syrians, Phoenicians, or Moabites!

The image of God as Lord of all nations and Judge of all nations, including his Chosen People, was an unbearable challenge to the self-image of the Jews.

Again, the Jewish belief in being the Chosen People was interpreted as a matter of favored status. God was conceived as owing the Jews something, because of his covenant with them. The accent was on Israel's special privileges at the neglect of their special responsibilities. And at a time of peace and unaccustomed prosperity, such a lopsided view of God's covenant with his people was easy to entertain.

But listen to Amos' version of the divine covenant and its application:

> *Listen, Israelites, to these words that the Lord addresses to you, to the whole nation which he brought up from Egypt: "For you alone have I cared among all the nations of the world: therefore will I punish you for all your iniquities."*            — Amos 3:1-2

And then Amos goes on to describe these iniquities and their consequence in detail, as for example:

> *Hear this, you who trample upon the needy, and bring the poor of the land to an end, saying "When will the new moon be over, that we may sell grain? And the sabbath, that we may offer wheat for sale, that we may make the ephah small and the shekel great, and deal deceitfully with false balances, that we may buy the poor for silver and the needy for a pair of sandals, and sell the refuse of the wheat?"*
>
> *The Lord has sworn by the pride of Jacob: "Surely I will never forget any of their deeds. Shall not the land tremble on this account, and every one mourn who dwells in it, and all of it rise like the Nile and sink again, like the Nile of Egypt?"*            — Amos 8:4-8

It seems rather obvious why Amaziah, God's high priest at Bethel, had to silence Amos! By voicing such biting criticism of his people, in God's name, Amos was in effect saying that being God's people would not protect them — that their underserved privilege would be revoked — that God would make use of pagans to judge and punish his Chosen People. Clearly, such an image of God challenged the entire self-image of the Jews!

But Amos does not stop there. He scoffs:

> *Bring your tithes within three days. Burn your thank-offering without leaven; announce, proclaim your free-will offerings; for you love to do what is proper, you men of Israel!* — Amos 4:4-5

And then Amos mounts his greatest attack, in the Lord's name:

> *I hate, I spurn your pilgrim feasts; I will not delight in your sacred ceremonies. When you present your sacrifices and offerings I will not accept them, nor look on the buffaloes of your shared offerings. Spare me the sound of your songs; I cannot endure the music of your lutes. Let justice roll down like a river and righteousness like an ever-flowing stream!* — Amos 5:21-24

In all the religions then known to the Jews, the gods demanded proper religious observance in return for their favor. Their concern with behavior, with social morality, was at best secondary.

The Jews themselves, however, had been covenanted to a quite different God from the beginning. This God, Jehovah, had been making social demands along with ritual demands right along. However, ritual demands were easier to satisfy than was the demand for social justice — the demand for compassion for the poor, the widow, the stranger, the handicapped. And in prosperous times, when the religious establishment fit into the economic and political establishment like a shapely hand into the right size glove, it was even easier to forget the social demands of God!

Thus Amos, by recalling Israel to the image of God as a God more concerned with social justice than with formal religion, challenged — and offended — their present self-image as God's people enjoying his uncritical favor thanks to their proper and lavish religious observance.

## The Relevance Of Amos

How does this ancient conflict, between Amos and Amaziah, between prophet and high priest, speak to us today? What are the durable elements in this patently dated story? What is the relevance of Amos, for us?

The difference between Amos' situation and our own is admittedly vast.

We have just about given up our "chosen people complex," though the notion that America as a nation is somehow entitled to special consideration from the Almighty dies hard. If there is one thing we are likely to have learned from Vietnam, it is that God plays no favorites with nations. Indeed, since the replacement of the Old Covenant with the New, the only community God can be said to have any corporate regard for is the Christian Church — a community which transcends all national, ethnic, or racial boundaries.

Thus we ought not to have any problem with accepting the impartiality of God in the world of nations, the fact that God does not favor any nation as a nation. And the insight that God is more concerned with justice and compassion than he is with the niceties of religious ritual and ceremonial, is as old as Moses, or Amos, and so widely accepted as to pass for a platitude.

But accepting something in theory, even as religious doctrine, does not mean that we are ready to apply it to ourselves, to live by it. If we really accepted the image of God which Amos proclaimed and Jesus confirmed, there would not be such an awful fuss every time a church body issues a statement — an unavoidably controversial statement — on a social problem! But that is what happens. So today, when we affirm our faith in the oneness of the Church of Jesus Christ by acknowledging in penitence our continuing denominational divisions, we owe it to ourselves to pause and acknowledge, perhaps with surprise, that far more stubborn division which divides us, within our denominations and even congregations, into

121

Christians who claim that there are *two gospels* and Christians who know that there is only *one*.

And this is where Amos becomes enormously relevant.

For Amos teaches us, first of all, that just as there is only one God, there is only one gospel. There is no "Social Gospel" and no "Personal Gospel." There is only one gospel, designed for real persons who are, by definition, persons in society.

God's concern is for persons. Social conditions foster or stunt our growth as persons. Therefore God is concerned — and bids us be concerned — with social conditions, with everything that either enhances or disfigures God's image in human beings.

It is silly — and tragic — for Christians to divide into camps labeled respectively "Personal Gospel" and "Social Gospel." Amos, centuries before the gospel, knew that there could be only one gospel!

From Amos also we can learn that we may do well to be modest. Amos himself was not modest. He had a clear word from the Lord — direct, specific. All he had to do was to proclaim it. We do not have such a word except in a very broad sense. We can be one hundred percent certain that treating a man as less than a man because of his race, is not just social dynamite but a moral outrage, a sin against God. But where we go from there is not equally clear. Neither Amos nor Jesus has any straight word about affirmative action.

Thus when a Social Pronouncement or a sermon affirms that a particular solution to a social problem is *the* Christian solution, we have every right to dissent. No one today has that kind of direct, specific revelation from the Lord!

Amos was not modest about his prophesying. He did not have to be. But we do. The next thing we can learn from Amos is that God is on the side of the underdog. In biblical times, this meant the widows, the orphans, the strangers, the handicapped, the sick, and, of course, the poor.

In our time, the list may be somewhat different. There certainly are significant additions, for example, the elderly who were not around in Amos' time, because few people lived beyond what we call early middle age.

Whatever the exact list in any age or place, the biblical witness to God's bias in favor of the underdog — the deprived, the disadvantaged — is unanimous: from Amos' indictment of the rich because of their oppression of the poor — through Jesus' Parable of the Judgment — to Saint John's picture of the judgment avenging upon haughty Rome the sorrows of all her victims.

Amos teaches us that the Church must be able to criticize the nation of which she is a part. When the Church is not free to speak critically to the political order, she ceases to be the Church — unless she goes underground. This is what happened in Nazi Germany. When Hitler called on Christians to conform uncritically to the new Nazi State, the majority obeyed — and thus ceased to be the Church. A minority, however, remained faithful by offering as much opposition as was possible, and by going underground. In our country, it is our sacred burden and God-given opportunity to be a prophetic Church — loyally, lovingly, redemptively critical of our government and other institutions.

But we also learn from Amos that the Church herself is not immune to the temptations to which the government and other institutions so readily succumb. Amos himself spoke out against the Church of his day as much as he spoke out in criticism of political and economic institutions and practices. Let us not forget that Amaziah was the High Priest at Bethel, one of the foremost churchmen in the Kingdom of Israel!

Finally, Amos reminds us that, as the Church of Jesus Christ, we must listen to, and even listen for, unlikely prophets — like himself, just in case God is trying to tell us something through someone from whom we expect no such thing. Amos was a layman, a quasi-foreigner, and a country bumpkin. But God was working through him, just as God may be working today through strange persons and groups — uncouth, lacking proper credentials.

Why was there such a fuss about Amos and his preaching? For the same reason there is a fuss every time the gospel is proclaimed in its singleness and wholeness, as both *personal and social*!

# Part Three

*Brainstorms*

# 1. Hosea

While only the first three chapters of the Book of Hosea are clearly autobiographical, his prophecies furnish a great deal of additional information about him.

The story of Hosea and Gomer, of course, presents a tantalizing and ultimately insoluble puzzle. Did Hosea seek out a prostitute in order to dramatize his message? Did he marry a "good girl" who deceived him and eventually became a prostitute? Did he ... and so on?

**The Four R's.** Hosea, a man of God, acts very much like God toward the straying Gomer. He agonizes over her *rebellion*, is broken-hearted over her *ruin*, seeks and gladly accepts her *repentance* and grants her full *restoration*. The story parallels the Father's way with the Prodigal Son (Luke 15). Hosea's name comes from the same root as Joshua and Jeshua/Jesus, meaning "Savior." The parallel is fitting.

**Broken Promises.** Gomer promised to marry Hosea "for better, for worse," and so on. She broke her promise, just as Israel was breaking her covenant with God. The more solemn the promise, the greater the misery or sadness that attends its betrayal. Are we, the Church, exacting too many promises (baptismal, marriage, membership, ordination) that people either cannot or do not even intend to keep? Could such promises be changed to annually renewable? Should they be?

**Is Goodness Boring?** Hosea was a good and righteous man but Gomer got so bored with him that she deceived him. The people of Israel often found the religion of the Baalim "more fun" than the religion of Yahweh. Is virtue, goodness, righteousness inevitably boring? Is it inevitable, in life as well as in the media, that "good news is no news"? Can goodness be exciting — and be kept that way?

**Those Poor PK's!** Hosea gave his children symbolically-charged names for the noblest prophetic reasons, but they would have to live with them for the rest of their lives! PK's (preacher's kids) used to have a tough row to hoe. Too many of them would grow up to become either pagans or preachers. Few were able to become their own, unique selves. Today we have begun to realize that, when God calls a man or woman to the ministry, no call is necessarily included for the children. Or even for the spouse!

**Great Harlots Of The Bible.** There is a sermon in Rahab, Gomer, and Mary Magdalene. Attitudes toward prostitution also changed a great deal from earlier permissiveness to later ostracism and, at least on paper, capital punishment. But these three women played, each in her own way, a significant part in God's action with his people. The point may be that, with God, no human being, no matter how marginal, is necessarily or finally excluded.

**Who, Really, Is Our God?** Hosea called his nation, Israel, a whore. What would happen to you if you, from the pulpit, called the United States a whore? Every church in our country has, and is expected to display, two flags. If you removed the Christian flag, no one might miss it. If you removed the national flag, even on the best-argued theological grounds, you would be unemployed on very short notice. Who, really, is our God?

**Can Love Go Too Far?** Hosea loved Gomer. Whatever she had been and however she treated him, he loved her, longed to have her back, searched for her everywhere, finally found her in a brothel and took her home as his loved and forgiven wife. He was the laughing-stock of the town. But it occurred to him that this was how God was dealing with Israel. That comforted him, because he was sure that the love of God could not go too far. "Master, how many times shall a man forgive...?"

**The Good Old Days.** Hosea's prophecies reveal a deep bias against cities. He longs for the wilderness — for the days of innocence, simplicity, faithfulness to God, communal solidarity which marked the people during their wanderings. Do we share his nostalgia sometimes? If so, do we have the option? Is there a way back to "Our Town"? Or, if there is not, what can we do to recover some of that lost quality of life?

# 2. Apollos

We know tantalizingly little about the ministry of Apollos, except that he probably played a far more important part in the Apostolic Church than is told in the references which mention him by name (Acts 18:24, 19:1; 1 Corinthians 1:10-13, 3:1-6, 16:12). According to Luther, he may be the author of the Epistle to the Hebrews. His Alexandrian Jewish background and his first class training in classical rhetoric give a good deal of plausibility to the Reformer's suggestion.

**A Great Catch.** On hearing Apollos hold forth in Ephesus, Aquila and Priscilla might just as well have sounded the alarm. Here was a dynamic speaker from the rival sect of John the Baptist beginning to undercut Paul's ministry. Aquila and Priscilla could have challenged him publicly. He would no doubt have defeated them in debate while being confirmed in his commitment to John. But Aquila and Priscilla took him aside, discreetly, without putting him on the spot — and he became an apostle of Jesus Christ. A great catch — and a lesson in method for all who wish to be evangelists.

**Half A Truth May Be Worse Than None.** Apollos "knew only the baptism of John" (the Baptist). His experience and training prepared him for the gospel. It also made it more likely for him to resist the gospel. "A little knowledge is a dangerous thing." That is why the mainline Protestant churches continue to insist on a fully-educated clergy. It is also why we offer as much adult education to laypersons as we can. Even a blank mind holds out more promise than a mind confused with half-truths.

**A Clash of Wills.** 1 Corinthians 16:12 can be read two ways. Apollos is in Ephesus with Paul, and Paul is telling the Christians in Corinth either that it is not Apollos' will to visit them now or that it is not God's will for Apollos to do so. A clash of wills between two persons is one thing. To decide what is God's will, for me or under any circumstances, is another. The motto of the Crusades was *Deus vult!* "God wills it!" Inquisitions, pogroms, conversions at sword's point have all been blessed by churches as the will of God. How can we tell what the will of God is? Or can we?

**Teachable Teacher.** Apollos was a highly-educated, brilliant preacher and teacher. He drew crowds and won converts for John the Baptist's sect. He was surely tempted to believe that he knew it all. But he managed to keep his eyes, his ears, and his mind open. He remained teachable, capable of further growth: the most needed qualification for teachers!

**What Is The Question?** Writer Gertrude Stein lay dying. Her companion, Alice Toklas, asked her, "Gertrude, what is the answer?" Feebly, Gertrude whispered, "What is the question?" We often give answers without knowing what the question is. Apollos did not make that mistake. He showed to the Jews at Ephesus "that the Christ was Jesus" (Acts 18:28). They had no problem believing in the Christ/Messiah. They just could not believe that Jesus of Nazareth, an obscure rabbi crucified as a rebel, could be he. Our problem is likely to be the opposite. We admire Jesus but are not sure that we need, or want, a Savior. The late Karl Menninger's book homes in on our problem with a question: *What Has Happened To Sin?*

**Whose Church?** As Christians, we are supposed to be transparent so that people looking at us should see through us and see only Christ. This does not come naturally. Paul had to deal with the problem in Corinth where factions had formed around favorite preachers like Apollos or Cephas/Peter or Paul himself. Next time you catch a pastor referring to the church he/she serves as "my church," say "Whoa! we are not yours. We are Christ's — and so are you!" Apollos had an extra hard time learning Christian transparency because he was a brilliant, magnetic speaker. But all of us must learn to keep in mind at all times whose Church the Church is.

# 3. Micah And The Levite

The story of Micah and the Levite and of the migration north of the tribe of Dan illustrates the wryly humorous comment with which the author or editor concludes the Book of Judges: "In those days there was no king in Israel: all the people did what was right in their own eyes." None of the characters in Judges 17 and 18 is admirable or even honorable. Deservedly or undeservedly, the whole tribe of Dan is depicted as treacherous. And, of course, just as the conquest of the Land of Promise is far from finished, monotheism is far from established: the worship of Yahweh is crudely mixed with the cult of other deities. Still, there are sermon nuggets buried in this rather unpromising material.

**Credentials.** After hiring the young Levite from Bethlehem, Micah, the rich farmer in the hill country of Ephraism, congratulated himself: "Now I know that the Lord will prosper me, because I have a Levite for a priest" (Judges 17:13). Micah had actually ordained one of his sons as priest of his private chapel, but now he had landed a real priest with the highest credentials: a Levite, a member of Israel's priestly tribe! Credentials are important. You would not want to entrust yourself to an un-credentialed surgeon, or architect, or watch repairman. But God often makes spectacular use of uncredentialed people, much to their own surprise and bewilderment. God called Moses who stuttered; Amos who was surely illiterate; Saul of Tarsus, who qualified impressively as persecutor of the "Jesus sect" but hardly as their advocate and leader. And what credentials, beyond his alleged Davidic lineage, did Jesus have for the office of universal Messiah?

**Promises.** Micah's mother had been saving 1,100 pieces of silver for a religious offering. Micah stole the money but, fearing her curse, returned it to her. Relieved, Micah's mother ordered a

133

statue of a household god from a silversmith for 200 pieces of silver, keeping 900 pieces for herself and thus cheating on her pledge. The story of Ananias and Sapphira (Acts 5:1-11) involves the same duplicity. Ananias and Sapphira had pledged their all, but then they welshed on their pledge, with fateful results. Integrity as well as common sense demands that we do not promise more than we truly intend to keep and are likely to be able to keep. What about all those marriage vows, when every other marriage ends in divorce? What about all those church pledges that fall short?

**Mother's Spoiled Baby.** The rich farmer Micah (Judges 17 and 18) is an unattractive character. There is irony in his very name: Micah, short for Micaiah, "who is like the Lord!" He steals from his mother. He is superstitious. He is self-satisfied, especially for landing a Levite to serve as his private priest. But how did Micah get that way? He lived in lawless times, yes. He probably lost his father early. But his mother spoiled him rotten! When he confesses to her that it was he who stole her money, she exclaims: "Blessed be my son to the Lord!" Now this might sound noble and forgiving, but next thing Micah's mother makes an offering of just 200 pieces of silver, instead of the 1,100 she had originally pledged. Thus between spoiling her boy and offering a shoddy role model, it is no wonder that she produces an unattractive son! Our parents powerfully influence our formation as persons. But does that entitle us to use them as alibis the rest of our adult life?

**Safely On The Payroll.** The young Levite was born to the priesthood but, as a man, he was interested only in his own well-being and career. When Micah invited him to become his private chaplain, he knew that he was getting a good deal. But when the Danites come, abusing Micah's hospitality and robbing him, the Levite barely protests. Rather he gladly accepts the "promotion" they offer him: to become chaplain of a whole tribe rather than of just one man. Whatever the Levite's shortcomings, both Micah and the Danites could count on him to stick to his religious duties and never, never challenge, let along criticize, his employer. Micah could do what he wanted. So could the Danites. The Levite would never take a stand against anything they might be doing. Are not too many congregations deprived of any moral guidance on significant public issues, because they do not want their pastor to "mix religion and politics," and because the pastor himself prefers to remain "safely on the payroll"?

# 4. Andrew

Being the brother of Simon Peter, the natural leader of the Twelve, could not have been easy for Andrew. Nor are his deeds half as well documented as those of his volcanic, mercurial brother. But this very neglect of Andrew by the Evangelists may heighten the challenge of his personality for preachers.

**Sibling Rivalry, Sibling Love.** After recalling and illustrating how Andrew was overshadowed by Peter, you might pass in review other biblical siblings: Cain and Abel, Esau and Jacob, Leah and Rachel, Joseph and his brothers, Martha and Mary, and by all means, James and John, the "Sons of Thunder." The accent should be on the ambivalence which marks and mars the relationship. You might conclude with a special intercession for brothers and sisters with whom we are at war — or just out of touch.

**Evangelist Par Excellence.** In John's Gospel there are three scenes in which Andrew plays a major part. In each of them he is bringing someone to Jesus. In John 1:35-42 it is his big brother, Simon, whom Jesus will rename Cephas or Peter, "Rock." In John 6:5-9, it is the little boy who is willing to share his lunch with 5,000 people, shaming the crowd into a feast of sharing. In John 12:20-23, it is the small group of Greeks, i.e., Gentiles studying Judaism with a view to conversion, who will find in Jesus the universal Messiah. Andrew's evangelistic method is simply exposing people to Jesus. Is there a better one?

**One Of The Twelve.** The disciples/apostles are often identified, individually, as "one of the Twelve." We know little about most of them except for their belonging to Jesus' inner circle. But you can tell a great deal about a man by the company he keeps, the organizations to which he belongs, the causes he supports. Much of who we are can be deduced from the cards we carry in our wallets. Andrew seemed content to be just "one of the Twelve." He did not join James and John when they asked the Master, foolishly, whether they might sit one at his right hand the other at his left, in the kingdom (Matthew 10:35-45). He did not register any jealousy when he was not permitted to witness Jesus' transfiguration (Matthew 17:1-8). He was satisfied to be a non-com in Jesus' army, in the shadow of General Peter. Has humility gone out of style?

**Called To Follow.** According to Matthew's account (4:18-19), Jesus called Andrew and Simon, fishermen by trade, while they were "casting a net into the sea." "Follow me," he said to them, "and I will make you fishers of men." At other times, he was calling men to become workers in his harvest, e.g., Matthew 9:37, "The harvest is plentiful but the laborers are few...." What would happen if we started challenging people to join in order to work with us for the Master instead of offering to "service" them? Might that not be a first step toward the renewal of our churches?

**The Cost of Conversion.** According to John 1:35-42, Peter and Andrew were both disciples of John the Baptist. When John met Jesus, he recognized him as the Messiah. "Behold the Lamb of God!" he exclaimed. In so doing, he virtually turned the brothers over to Jesus. But this is not how it usually goes. Becoming a Christian by leaving another religious community is likely to exact a price: from family conflict to ostracism and even martyrdom. Are we showing appropriate understanding and patience with non-Christians — whether in Asia, Africa or on the fringes of our own congregation — when they are hesistant to take the plunge into the waters of baptism?